The GUINNESS Book of
Trees

Britain's Natural Heritage

The GUINNESS Book of

TREES

Esmond & Jeanette Harris

Illustrations by Vanessa Luff

GUINNESS SUPERLATIVES LIMITED
2 CECIL COURT, LONDON ROAD, ENFIELD, MIDDLESEX

© Guideway Publishing Ltd 1981

Designed and produced by Guideway Publishing Ltd,
Willow House, 27-49 Willow Way, London SE26

Published in 1981 by Guinness Superlatives Ltd,
2 Cecil Court, London Road, Enfield, Middlesex EN2 6DJ

Guinness is a registered trademark of
Guinness Superlatives Ltd

Harris, Esmond and Jeanette
The Guinness book of trees.
(Britain's natural heritage).
1. Trees – Great Britain
I. Title   II. Series
582'.16'0941   QK488

ISBN 0-85112-303-1

Printed by Morrison & Gibb Ltd, Edinburgh

The publishers wish to thank the following for their permission
to reproduce photographs:

Front cover: (Maple glade, Westonbirt, Gloucestershire.)
Royal Forestry Society.
Heather Angel: 51,55,57,59,61,65,69,73,77,79,81,83,85,87,91,
93,95,97,99,101,103,105,111,113,115,117,119,121,123,125,127,
131,133,137,139,141,145,147,149.
Elspeth Harris: 67,143
Scott Leathart: 75,129
Maurice Nimmo (A-Z Botanical Ltd): 53,63,71,89,107,109,135.

Contents

Introduction

What do we really mean by 'heritage'? Broadly speaking, it is all that we inherit from the past. In the case of a long-established family, heritage includes material possessions and traditions, some of which have been handed down through many generations while others are more recent acquisitions added by immediate ancestors. When we refer to our national heritage, we mean the art, music, literature, architecture, institutions and traditions that make our country unique and what it is today. Our national heritage has come from a fusion of diverse peoples and cultures throughout our history, from the moment when man first invaded Britain, thousands of years ago, to the present day; from our neolithic forebears, through the Celts, Romans, Norse, Anglo-Saxon and Norman invasions to the more peaceful infiltrations, such as the Flemish in East Anglia as well as the acceptance of the House of Hanover as our Royal Family. Britain has added to her diversity through all these influences. As a result we have a history and traditions envied by much of the world. This is our national heritage.

The effect or value of some new influences is not always apparent at the time, and what is desirable to keep and what to reject is a matter of personal preference. To some, Victorian architecture is hideous but certain of its qualities may determine design in the future. Beethoven in his day was regarded as a discordant composer and not any better than some of his contempories but his music has withstood the test of time. We cannot tell at a particular moment just what the future holds and so must not discard any part of our heritage too freely.

Our natural heritage includes the animals, plants, birds and trees that have been with us for many thousands of years as well as the more recent invasions of others, both natural and man-assisted, that continue today. Not all of these invasions have been welcome ones, for example, the brown rat or Dutch elm disease which so recently swept through the countryside. Welcome or unwelcome, all are part of our natural heritage and, as inheritors of it, it is our responsibility to preserve and improve as much as possible so that a wealth of plant and animal life is handed down to future generations.

Our tree heritage has varied in numbers and diversity throughout the ages. A wide variety of trees grew here before the Ice Age, but they were devastated by the cold and the ice sheets that covered the land during that long period. As the ice finally retreated, plant and animal life in Europe moved north again, the trees more slowly than animals and short-lived plants. The origin in Britain of some trees is debatable, the question being whether they arrived naturally after the Ice Age or more recently assisted by man. One fact is certain, however: once the land-bridge with Europe had broken, forming the English Channel, further additions to our tree heritage were all man-assisted, a process of adding to our flora which continues to the present day. Thus, of the 1500 species of trees that are growing in Britain now, only about 35 are considered to have arrived here without the aid of man.

There is a widespread feeling prevalent today that only trees that are 'natural' in Britain should be encouraged and planted. For some unexplained reason, this concept is not proposed in other fields of natural history. The ornithologist is only too glad to add further birds to the British list, their passport normally resting on their ability to cross the sea unaided. However, the capercaillie, pheasant and red-legged partridge are among some of the birds introduced by man. Are they to be regarded as undesirable? About one-third of our wild land animals, excluding bats and seals whose access is not restricted by the English Channel, have been introduced by man, either deliberately or accidentally but are nevertheless all accepted. Indeed it is sometimes suggested that animals that have become extinct should be re-introduced such as

the wild boar and beaver so that the variety of our
mammals could be further increased.

In the same way, many plants that are now regarded as
part of the British flora came here through man's agency.
Some came as seeds mixed by accident with the seeds of
wanted species; while others were originally cultivated in
gardens and have escaped and naturalised themselves. An
example of the latter is a musk (monkey flower) which
was originally grown in gardens but is now common in
wet places throughout Britain.

How many early tree introductions were accidental we will
never know. It has been suggested that sweet chestnut was
introduced accidentally, the nuts having been discarded
on refuse heaps in Roman times; others hold the view that
it was introduced deliberately and planted with the
intention of providing food for the Roman army. What is
known is that the Roman soldiers were fed on a flour
obtained by crushing the nuts. Now sweet chestnut
flourishes throughout southern Britain. From the
sixteenth century onwards, written records of trees are
available and we know from these not only when
particular trees were introduced but in many cases by
whom. Many of these trees are now such a familiar part
of the countryside that it is not often realised that they
were introduced. For instance, the horse chestnut is
known to more people than most of our native trees.
Larch, too, can be found throughout Britain. However
the date of introduction of both is known and recorded.
Our tree heritage includes many such trees.

Our Tree Heritage

Wherever man goes, his influence on the landscape becomes apparent and the introductions by him of plants, trees and other forms of life follow. This pattern is not peculiar to Britain. One has only to look at the devastation caused by rabbits in Australia and the results of pine blister rust, accidentally introduced from Europe, in the United States of America, to see the worst effects; the successful introductions of potatoes and rubber to countries outside their native South America, to see the benefits. Imagine Britain without the beauty of exotic ornamental trees, or any introduced garden plants or crops. Should an introduced tree, such as Sitka spruce, be condemned because it grows better than native trees and is of economic benefit? In agriculture, animals and crops are continually being introduced and bred for better economic performance but no one seriously suggests we should return to only our native crop plants and animals.

One of the arguments often put forward for increasing the planting of native species is to encourage wildlife and to conserve natural ecosystems, by which is meant particular forms of vegetation and the animals associated with them. This presents special problems as such situations have evolved over a long period and are not always naturally stable as they are continually evolving. Management is necessary to maintain them at the desired level if a particular stage is to be preserved. An example of this are areas of downland set aside for the protection of rare orchids. Unless these downs are grazed, they soon become invaded by shrubs and trees so that conditions are no longer suitable for the orchids. In the past, these areas were grazed by rabbits before they were decimated by myxamatosis and by sheep, whose grazing was discontinued for economic reasons. To maintain this ecosystem in a condition suitable for orchids, the area must be actively managed by man.

When the planting of native, rather than introduced, trees is proposed to encourage wildlife, oak woodland is usually quoted as supporting more wildlife than other types of woods. When it is remembered that oak has been the climax vegetation in Britain for thousands of years, it is not surprising that the number and diversity of insect and other species is greater in such woods. There is evidence, however, that many birds and insects are not necessarily confined to dependence on a particular tree species and, given the opportunity, they will exploit new habitats provided by plantations of introduced trees. Plantations of the introduced Corsican pine have been found to have almost as many species of birds in them as those of native Scots pine. It has also been found that plantations of young hardwoods do not contain larger numbers of birds than those of conifers.

To maintain, therefore, that only native species should be encouraged is not coming to terms with reality, either from a conservation point of view or an economic one. Our tree heritage has been increased and diversified and will continue to be so. Many opportunities for tree planting exist today which require special considerations and our native trees cannot always provide suitable candidates. There is a great demand for trees to ameliorate obtrusive modern buildings and line city streets. The Lombardy poplar, although not a native tree, is a popular and graceful tree for the first situation, while trees withstanding drought conditions and intense light are needed for the second, such as some of the cherries and rowans from the Far East. The planting of coal tips is an important way of improving the landscape and exotic trees such as the grey alder and false acacia have proved eminently suitable for this purpose. Most people, too, would choose a quick-growing introduced conifer for a shelter belt or hedge where rapid results are required rather than the more slow-growing native species. Economic considerations mean that trees are needed for timber and it is an indisputable fact that many of our introduced conifers excel in this respect, providing higher quality timber and in a very much shorter time than our native species.

Our tree heritage thus consists of a wide diversity of species and how we use it and manage it is a challenge. We must understand the best ways to integrate different species into the landscape to enrich it visually, gain economic benefit, encourage wildlife and provide areas for relaxation and refreshment of the spirit for town dwellers. Our tree heritage is an immensely complex inheritance which should be cherished for the benefit of future generations. To be successful it must be taken as a living and dynamic whole which is evolving all the time. To choose to preserve beech but exclude sycamore, for instance, is ecologically untenable and would deny future generations the opportunities of choice. Indeed, it has been said that 'we do not inherit the earth but merely borrow it from our children'. This sentiment should always be borne in mind.

The Pioneers

Thousands of years ago Britain was part of a great land mass which eventually broke up into the continents that we know today. These land divisions gradually separated, drifting apart and are still doing so. The climate and physical conditions of each area differed, giving rise to complex changes in the plant and animal life contained within them. Two of the main factors causing these changes are of particular importance. One is the altering of climate and physical conditions. Relatively small alterations in these may, in a short time, dramatically favour one species and destroy another, while major alterations may have catastrophic effects. The disappearance of the dinosaur is thought to be due to such a major change. Secondly, side by side with these major and minor fluctuations, plants and animals are constantly endeavouring to reach an equilibrium within the habitat as it exists at a particular moment and to maintain stable conditions.

Once conditions in Britain became suitable towards the end of the major geological period known as the palaeozoic, the earliest true trees to appear were the ancestors of present-day conifers. The maidenhair tree and its relatives occurred then and the former is now the only living descendant. In the next period, the mesozoic, conditions particularly favourable to the evolution of trees and conifers began to appear. The major change they achieved was adaption to drier conditions by improving reproductive methods, so that trees were no longer dependent on water for fertilisation to take place as their immediate ancestors had been. Toward the end of this period the flowering trees—often called 'hardwoods'—began to appear.

At the beginning of the last major period—the cainozoic—which includes the Ice Age and also brings us to the present day, there is evidence from fossil records of a wide range of trees growing in Britain. These included the maidenhair tree, araucaria (monkey-puzzle), sciadopitys, redwood, swamp cypress and yew. From among the flowering trees, tulip tree, walnut, plane, laurels, fig, Indian bean and the southern beeches were present in Britain. As conditions changed so did the tree species and, in the drier, cooler conditions preceding the Ice Age, trees growing in Britain included Norway spruce (the Christmas tree), Scots pine, yew, hornbeam, hazel, birch, alder, beech, oak, elm, rowan, blackthorn, hawthorn, maple, alder, buckthorn and dogwood.

Although the Ice Age is usually spoken of as if it was a continuous phase, it was in fact a series of major climatic fluctuations. The number of actual glacial periods and their extent is open to question and so too is the extent and duration of the inter-glacials in between. As far as Britain is concerned, the last glacial period, which was also the most extensive, occurred over 17 000 years ago when glaciers covered all except the extreme south of Britain. During the fluctuations in the extent of the ice sheets, the vegetation also ebbed and flowed according to climate. Although now regarded as exotics, Norway spruce and European silver fir were part of the vegetation in the warmer periods. With the last major glaciation, it is usually considered that trees and shrubs were all wiped out although small plants, known as arctic-alpines, survived on high areas not covered by the ice. At this time Britain was still joined to the continental land mass so that, when the ice retreated, vegetation moved north again from ice-free areas as conditions became suitable. Colonisation of the bare areas left by the ice was at first by short-lived species, often with light wind-blown seeds which spread quickly and were capable of living on denuded areas with poor soil—the 'pioneers'. The same or similar species are the pioneers of ecological succession today when an area is cleared of vegetation and natural colonisation takes place. These pioneers are usually short-lived and in many cases are able to fix nitrogen from the soil-air with the help of bacteria or increase the uptake of phosphorus with the aid of fungi, so that they can survive on poor soils. They gradually enrich the soil and also provide shelter for the seedlings of longer-lived trees which cannot tolerate such harsh conditions but can grow in more shady situations. As these trees grow up, they in turn eventually shade out the pioneer species which require plenty of light for their growth.

Our knowledge of the tree species that have been present since the retreat of the ice is based chiefly on a technique known as pollen analysis. The male flowers of conifers and flowering trees produce pollen, the grains of which are distinctive for a species or genus and their remains can be found preserved in the peat of bogs and lakes. These pollen grains can be dated by their position in the peat layers and a picture of vegetation conditions built up from the proportion of pollen of various plant and tree species. A high proportion of plant pollen to tree pollen indicates open conditions and the in-

AGE	PERIOD		CLIMATE	TREES PRESENT	MAN
	Pre-glacial		Warm	Ginkgo, sciadopitys, redwood, monkey-puzzle, swamp cypress, tulip tree, walnut, plane, laurel, fig, Indian bean, southern beech.	
	Pre-glacial		Colder	Norway spruce, Scots pine, yew, hazel, birch, hornbeam, beech, alder, oak, elm, rowan, field maple, hawthorn.	
	Glacial		Very cold	No record.	
	Inter-glacial		Cold to warm	Norway spruce, silver fir.	
20 000 BC	Glacial		Very cold	No record. Trees thought to have gone.	River drift man. Neanderthal man.
	Inter-glacial		Cold to warm	No record.	Aurignacian man.
15 000 BC	Glacial		Very cold	All trees thought to have gone.	
10 000 BC	I	Early Dryas	Cold	Dwarf willow and birch on tundra. Juniper.	
9000 BC	II	Alleroid	Warmer but cool	Birch, aspen, juniper, Scots pine.	Palaeolithic man (food gatherers and hunters).
8000 BC	III	Later Dryas	Cold	Dwarf willow, birch on tundra. Dwarf birch.	
	IV	Pre-boreal	Continental climate	Willows, juniper, rowan, birch, pine, bird cherry, ash.	Fire used as tool to clear forests.
7000 BC	V	Boreal	Warm Continental climate	Extensive pine and hazel. Elm, oak, small-leafed lime, alder appear.	Mesolithic man (hunters, fishers).
5500 BC	VI	Boreal	Warm Continental climate	Extensive pine and hazel. Alder and lime increase. Oak, elm (wych). In neolithic charcoal: yew, crab apple, poplar, whitebeam, buckthorn.	Man fells trees with axes and begins to herd animals. Neolithic man herding some domestic animals and cultivating some crops.
2500 BC	VII	Atlantic	Coastal climate with mild winters and high rainfall	Oak, elm and lime increase. Hawthorn, holly, cherry.	Bronze Age.
400 BC	VIII	Sub-boreal	Climate more Continental	Oak/ash forests. Elm and lime decrease. Beech and hornbeam appear about 2000 BC. Charcoals include: hawthorn, service tree, elm, plum, cherry blackthorn. Probable introduction of: walnut, white poplar, sweet chestnut, peach, apricot, quince, fig, medlar.	Extensive cultivation for agriculture. Forest clearance. Iron Age. Romans.
	IX	Sub-Atlantic	Cool climate with cooler summers	Beech/hornbeam forest. Less oak.	

fluence of clearing by man can be assumed in areas where forest was previously the main vegetation.

Interpretation of pollen records is difficult for a number of reasons. Some species, especially hazel, may produce abundant pollen thus giving a false impression of its importance. Similarly alder may appear abundant because its pollen is not carried very far and is more likely to fall into wet areas where it will be preserved. Some pollens are carried by the wind for greater distances than others and this too may affect the apparent abundance of different species shown by the pollen records. Other pollens do not preserve well and these include those of aspen and the maples, including sycamore. The absence of such pollen does not necessarily mean that the trees were not present and other evidence in the form of preserved seeds, twigs or wood must be taken into account.

With the retreat of the ice, conditions were very like those of the tundra in the north of Canada and Siberia today, with very wet conditions and little vegetation. In this period the first trees to invade were birch and willow, followed by aspen, juniper and sea buckthorn. As conditions became warmer, Scots pine, hazel and bird cherry appear in the peats though the area of open ground was still considerable and the tree cover was still light. This is indicated by the high proportion of plant pollen compared to tree pollen. Conditions continued to become warmer and the area covered by forest extended. Although pine and hazel were the main forest species at this time, oak, small-leafed lime, alder and elder appeared. The species of elm present cannot be distinguished by their pollen and it is considered that the elm represented was wych elm as this species tolerates more exacting conditions than other elms. Oaks and birches, too, cannot with any certainty be separated by their pollen into their respective species.

The climate continued to become warmer and wetter with the forest cover extending rapidly at the expense of open areas. As well as the increase of the dominant pine/hazel forest, alder became abundant indicating wet conditions. It is considered that these warm, wet conditions were precipitated by the severence of Britain's land connection with the Continent which took place at about this time (6000 to 8000 years ago). Before this, the climate had been much colder and Continental in type, favouring pine forest; but once Britain became an island and more influenced by the Gulf Stream, the warmer, wetter conditions encouraged the spread of broadleafed deciduous trees. The removal of the land-bridge at this time halted the invasion of Britain by those animals and plants whose methods of distribution did not allow them to cross an ever-increasing water barrier as the Channel widened. The general sinking of the land also cut Ireland off from the mainland of Britain with the result that only two-thirds of British plants are found there with even fewer trees and animals. Evidence for the land sinking is found in submerged forests, especially of oak and pine, found round the coasts of Britain.

With the warmer, wetter conditions, oak forest became the main forest cover in most of Britain except for the north. It was towards the end of this period that man began to make his influence felt upon the landscape. As a hunter and gatherer of nuts and fruits, man had invaded Britain in about 20000 BC during one of the inter-glacial periods. He probably lived on the arctic animals here at that time, including mammoth and reindeer. After the ice retreated, man gradually increased in numbers and there is evidence of him using axes to fell trees as early as 7000 BC. At about 2500 BC, a significant change occurred. From then onwards considerable immigration took place in successive waves although the land-bridge to the Continent had gone. Farming by keeping domestic animals and raising crops heralded the beginning of man's settlement in one area and the resulting impact on its vegetation. The keeping of domestic animals meant the clearance of forest and maintenance of open areas for grazing. From that time, the influence of man on our tree heritage becomes of increasing significance. The table on page 13 sets out some of the trees present in Britain before the Ice Age and those that have been identified by pollen analysis and other remains, from the time that the ice retreated until the beginning of recorded history in Britain.

With the clearing of trees and use of wood by man, another method of establishing the presence of trees is available. Where man used fire, especially for charcoal burning, tree charcoals have been preserved and can be collected, dated and identified from archaeological sites. Among the species that have been found in this way are crab apple, whitebeam and poplar.

At about 2000 BC beech begins to appear in the pollen records, long after the Channel was formed. The possibility that its introduction was by man is irresistible as its nuts are a useful food for animals and were eaten by man as well. It is known from European pollen records that its natural spread from Ice-Age refuges in the Balkans and south-west Europe was very slow compared with other species.

These records show that northern Germany and France were not reached by beech until about 6000 BC when the Channel was already forming.

It is unrealistic to be dogmatic about whether certain trees arrived unaided in Britain. All that can be said is that a number of species have been here for such a long time that they have become part of our landscape. It becomes a meaningless academic distinction to class some as native and others not. Trees of importance as food sources, both to man and his animals, such as beech, crab apple and pear could well have been introduced by man, or their spread north accelerated by his activities. Early man certainly introduced agricultural crops such as cereals which are not native to Britain and it is likely that he introduced some trees as well.

The question, therefore, of what constitutes a truly native tree is a vexed one as the evidence for many trees is inconclusive and becomes a matter of opinion. The much maligned sycamore falls into this category and could well have been here for much longer than is usually admitted, especially when it is remembered that maples (of which the sycamore is one) form an important constituent of natural forests in other temperate areas. As its pollen does not preserve easily, the tree could well have been here for a long time. Even spruce, generally regarded as introduced from Europe in the sixteenth century, appears as timber on archaeological sites in Shetland dating from neolithic times. The usual explanation is that building material was collected from driftwood, but, as northern Scotland and Scandinavia, where Norway spruce is native, were joined in post-glacial times, some spruce may have been growing in northern Britain after the Ice Age. The line to be drawn between the natural pioneers and those trees which may or may not have arrived unaided cannot be definite. At no stage of history can we draw hard and fast lines between cultures and traditions. We do not in other branches of natural history so neither should we for trees.

The Decline of the Pioneers

The tree pioneers were at first little affected by man the pioneer, as he was present in such small numbers. Exactly when and to what extent his activities caused changes we will never know, but wherever man goes he modifies natural conditions. It is generally assumed that man was of no importance as an influence on the landscape before he became a cultivator of crops rather than a hunter and gatherer of food. Even this change was gradual and all these activities were integrated into the primitive economy, certain aspects being more important in some areas than others. As a hunter, gatherer and herder, man in small numbers could spread his activities over large areas. Even today, tribes dependent on herding animals, both semi-domesticated (reindeer) and domesticated (cattle and sheep), graze their animals over extensive tracts of land. Until recently the tribes of Iran travelled hundreds of miles between winter and summer grazing, and primitive man almost certainly followed the migrating animal herds as they moved north and south with the seasons. Indeed, early man probably moved about extensively until increasing population and territorial demarcation prevented this. Once the tool of fire was available, it surely did not take long before it was used to burn off forest and scrub to encourage grazing in order to attract wild animals and eventually for domesticated ones. Felling of mature trees with flint tools is known to have taken place as early as 7000 BC and trees may also have been ring-barked to clear the forest. On such areas, fire would then have been invaluable to keep them clear by preventing regeneration.

At about 2500 BC waves of immigration increased the population and cultivation increased significantly enough to have an impact on the forest. A change to extensive open areas shows clearly in the pollen records. It is generally acknowledged that these immigrants were primarily farmers from Europe, but it must be remembered that their influence was chiefly in the south. The immigrants brought with them cereals to cultivate and inadvertently mixed with the grains many of our arable weed seeds. It is possible that they may have introduced useful food trees such as the wild plum and pear. At about this time, the climate became drier; this is considered to have assisted man to establish grazing and cultivation on the more thinly wooded upland areas in the south, such as the North and South Downs. More woods were also felled to provide charcoal with which to smelt copper and tin as bronze had now become important for tool-making and ornaments.

At about 1000 BC the plough took over from the hoe as a method of cultivation and larger fields were required, resulting in more tree felling. To maintain the increasing population herds of domesticated animals rose in numbers and grazing areas increased at the expense of forest. This is shown by the dramatic rise in the proportion of herb pollen to tree pollen in the records. Heavy grazing by domestic animals prevented regeneration of tree seedlings and maintained grazing areas. Man, too, cut grassland and scrub to provide bedding and fodder which also prevented the regeneration of tree seedlings.

As the population continued to rise, the introduction of iron tools made clearing the forest easier and the number of settlements increased, especially in the lowlands. By Roman times, Britain was still well wooded in the north and west but the south had seen considerable reduction of forest cover. To the Romans, the smelting of iron, copper and lead was important and meant the felling of trees for charcoal. Mining was already important as far afield as the Weald of Kent, Cornwall, the Mendips, Yorkshire, Wales and the Lake District so that woodlands in these areas began to feel the intense influence of man. This pressure has been relentless ever since.

With the removal of tree cover, there also began the steady deterioration of the soil. The continual taking of crops, and removal of soil nutrients by livestock in the form of meat and milk, broke the nutrient cycle that occurs under forest conditions. Removal of tree cover also accelerated leaching of nutrients out of the soil because the water passed through the soil more rapidly, carrying them away into rivers and lakes. Soil deterioration from this cause was more rapid in the higher rainfall areas in the west and north.

By 1086 it is clear that two-thirds of the virgin woodland had been removed. The *Domesday Book* provides the first census of both woods and man and gives an indication of the pressures on woodland at this time. For many centuries, trees had provided building materials to house man, especially in areas where stone was not easily available, and firewood to keep him warm. It had also built him boats, carts, tools and provided fibres for ropes and floor covering. It was an important source of animal food by providing leaves as forage and nuts such as acorns. Grazing and eating of seed

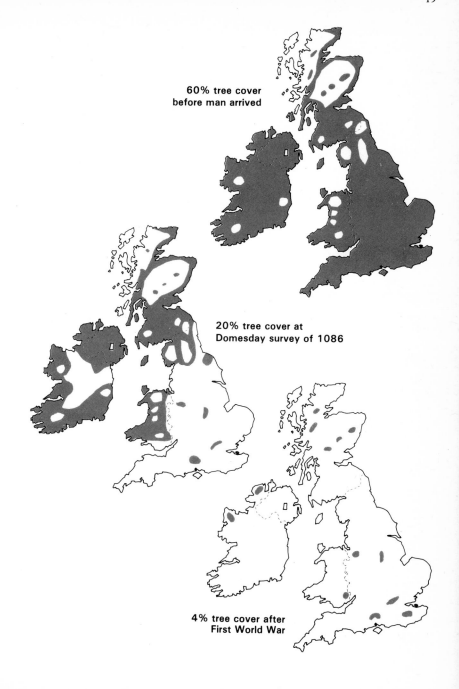

60% tree cover
before man arrived

20% tree cover at
Domesday survey of 1086

4% tree cover after
First World War

prevented the woodland regenerating and these areas in many cases became known as 'village wastes'.

All these activities in woodland became regulated and, by the Norman Conquest, especially in the southern part of Britain, each village had its own wooded area to supply its inhabitants. Even then they could not go into the woods and take what they liked. The removal of produce was strictly allocated and controlled and the number of grazing animals per person limited. In addition to village regulations, royal laws also existed, especially in relation to hunting deer and many areas were designated as Royal Forests. Of these only a few now remain, administered by the Forestry Commission, the most well known being the Forest of Dean and the New Forest. In Scotland forest laws also existed. By the eleventh century, woodland was already sparse in the southern part of that country. Here some of the great abbeys, such as Melrose, cultivated large areas of land and pastured sheep. Much timber had been used for the building of churches and, in 1457, laws were passed to encourage tree planting.

In England a law was passed in 1483 by Edward IV which allowed enclosure of woods against grazing animals for seven years so that coppicing could be practised. This gave trees, usually sweet chestnut, hornbeam and hazel, time to grow a good harvest of poles for use as fencing, firewood, charcoal and building materials. Hazel was used for many purposes, including wattle-and-daub for houses, mainly for the poorer members of the population. Frameworks of hazel provided a base on which to put the clay and these were set in between the structural oak timbers of the house. Much forest produce was cut into fuelwood, in four foot (1.2m) lengths, which was piled into stacks (on the sides of rides) eight feet (2.5m) long which were called 'cords'. The amount of wood consumed in this way was considerable. The regular cutting of woodlands for these needs became known as coppicing (such areas became 'copses') and where large trees, especially oak, were also allowed to grow up, the practice was known as 'coppice with standards'. As these large trees had plenty of light and space, they branched freely and spread; the crooked timber thus produced naturally was ideal for beams and rafters. Later such open-grown oaks were of value for ship building which became very important from Tudor times onwards until displaced by iron. It has been said that 2000 oaks were required to provide the timber needed to build an Elizabethan galleon. Another method of management that was practised was 'pollarding', that is, coppicing the tree at head height above the reach of grazing animals so fencing was unnecessary. By the sixteenth century increasing amounts of wood were used for charcoal, especially for iron smelting (cannons and anchors), brick and glass-making and in the manufacture of gunpowder. As the wood was bulky and expensive to transport, charcoal was produced in the forest and then carried to where it was required—a practice continued until well into this century in some areas. Much of the oak woodland in the north and west was used for charcoal and the bark for tannin. In fact, by Elizabethan times most woodland had felt the hand of man and much of the scrub oak in the north and west today is all that survives of original oak forest after centuries of cutting and unrestricted grazing. Rabbits, introduced by the Normans, as well as the steady rise in numbers of sheep, wool having been important since mediaeval times, must by now have been adversely affecting regeneration and laws were passed by Elizabeth I to restrict the cutting of trees.

The shortage of wood meant that attention now turned to the Highlands of Scotland where the only great reserves were left. Some was cut for smelting and much for naval purposes, especially Scots pine for ships' masts which was floated down the rivers. This exploitation continued until the middle of the nineteenth century and large areas became grazing for sheep and for red deer, which had now moved from the forests to the hills. Grazing by these animals prevented regeneration of trees. Shortage of timber had resulted in its importation, from the Baltic, as early as the twelfth century into England and by the thirteenth century into Scotland.

The continued destruction of woodland, and the realisation that this could not continuue, came to a head in the seventeenth century. It was then that John Evelyn wrote his famous *Silva, or a Discourse of Forest Trees* which was the first attempt to collect together information on trees and forestry practice. From this book it is evident that a considerable amount was already known about trees by this time and many common-sense forestry principles were already being practised.

At about the same time, side by side with the destruction of woodlands, there began a movement in the reverse direction of planting trees, which gained momentum in the succeeding decades. Much of this planting was ornamental in parks and 'policies' (in Scotland), providing visual amenity and shelter round the large houses now favoured by those who could afford them. Landowners, such as the Dukes of Atholl, established extensive plantations. Much of this planting became possible after the acts of enclosure which permitted landowners to take in and fence land. Enclosure, especially in southern Britain, also marked the beginning of a more efficient agriculture where crops could be fenced and protected and animals bred along particular lines by selection—a process impossible to achieve before when animals mixed indiscriminately on common grazing. With the enclosure of fields, miles of hawthorn hedges were planted, still a characteristic feature of much of our countryside.

Suddenly, however, the demand for certain types of wood fell. The use of coal instead of wood for fuel reduced the demand for firewood and the building of iron ships destroyed the market for open-grown oak. The availability of imports of timber from abroad, especially in the late nineteenth century, reduced the amount of money spent on planting by landowners, as it then became more profitable to invest in trade and commerce. By the end of the nineteenth century it was appreciated officially that timber resources had fallen to a dangerously low level and the Office of Woods, Forests and Land Revenues was formed. This body began afforestation at Hafod Fawr in North Wales in 1899, which was the first attempt to replenish national reserves. This was followed by planting at Inverliever in Scotland in 1909. Experiments to test the suitability of deodar and Douglas fir as commercial trees were also carried out in the New Forest.

One last onslaught was still to be made, especially on the new woods planted by the far-sighted landowners of the eighteenth century. The First World War saw millions of acres fall to the axe to supply the country with pit props for the coal mines, for industry and to keep the vital Royal Navy at sea. At this time the forest cover of Britain reached an all-time low of four per cent of the land surface, the lowest in Europe—a position which we still hold.

After the First World War the Forestry Commission was set up on the recommendation of the Acland Committee to try and rectify the situation by building up the nation's timber reserves, a task which continues today. The destruction of the pioneers had been finally halted. Although virgin forest untouched by the hand of man no longer exists in Britain, a few areas are left which have always carried forest. Although cut by man and grazed by his animals, these still retain unique ecological conditions that cannot be reproduced except by the passage of time. These remnants of the pioneers are part of our heritage that must be preserved for our successors.

The Welcome Aliens

Between the pioneer trees that re-colonised Britain after the Ice Age and the beginning of written records concerning the introduction of trees, there exists an area of uncertainty and speculation. As archaeological techniques and investigations improve and extend knowledge, pieces are fitted into the complex jigsaw puzzle of those times which is still very far from complete.

One factor that can be taken as certain is that, during this early period, human nature and actions were very much the same as they are today. In his explorations of new areas, man takes familiar objects and food with him, not knowing what may be available ahead in the unknown. Even when settlement has taken place, contact is kept up with the areas of origin.

Primitive man, too, probably continued to have contact with his areas of origin by trade routes, new ideas and imports travelling along such pathways. In this way, many fruit trees, originally developed in south-east Asia, must have reached Britain. Apples and pears were important food items in neolithic times, pears being sliced and dried for use in the winter. No doubt, too, the art of brewing drink from fruits was developed early. By the Bronze Age, the apples and pears being grown were much larger than before and must have been imported and improved varieties introduced from south-east Europe. Plums, too, are usually considered to have originated in the same area from a cross between blackthorn and myrobalan or cherry plum. By Celtic times, just before the Roman conquest of Britain, the idea of growing fruit in orchards had been accepted and developed. Crab apple and wild pear, from which these cultivated fruits were derived, are both found in the wild in Britain but their date of arrival is not known and wild pear is considered by some to have originated from cultivated trees that became naturalised long ago. The same may be true of crab apple. These fruit trees and other useful trees may all have been introduced by man or their range extended by being spread artificially by him, even if already growing here in the wild. Blackthorn, hawthorn, elder, cherries, beech, oak and hazel are all species for which man has found a use from very early times, both for food and other purposes. The thorns of blackthorn and hawthorn provided thorny barriers, either living or dead, for the protection of domestic flocks from wild animals, while hazel provided fencing, building material and food.

A number of trees have been considered Roman introductions but they could well have been introduced long before. These include the myrobalan plum and the true service tree, among those producing fruit. The true service tree is often accepted as a native although it is not now found in the wild. Other trees whose time of arrival in Britain is open to speculation include Swedish whitebeam, white poplar (here earlier but also much imported in the seventeenth century), grey poplar (now thought to be a hybrid between white poplar and aspen), some elms and limes and the disputed sycamore.

The Romans grew a wide range of fruit trees in Italy and are usually credited with the introduction of many of these to Britain, though some species may have been introduced before the Roman invasion. Among the fruit trees usually considered to be of Roman introduction are the walnut, peach, apricot, quince, fig, medlar and, possibly, mulberry. However, pollen grains of walnut have also been found on Iron-Age sites. Sweet chestnut is thought to have been introduced by the Romans as it is known that on the Continent the army was fed on flour made from the nuts. Another suggestion is that the nuts from food stores were thrown on rubbish heaps and germinated there.

Origins of species introduced into Britain

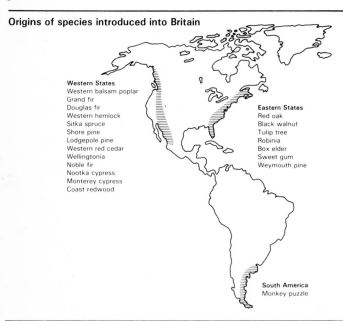

Western States
Western balsam poplar
Grand fir
Douglas fir
Western hemlock
Sitka spruce
Shore pine
Lodgepole pine
Western red cedar
Wellingtonia
Noble fir
Nootka cypress
Monterey cypress
Coast redwood

Eastern States
Red oak
Black walnut
Tulip tree
Robinia
Box elder
Sweet gum
Weymouth pine

South America
Monkey-puzzle

In addition to those of a purely economic nature, the Romans introduced plants and trees which reminded them of their native Italy, just as colonial settlers in India grew the English rose. It has been suggested that these included Italian cypress, sweet bay and the Oriental plane and that, without the care of cultivation, they died out after the Romans left Britain. The purely ornamental introductions would have had no place in the following centuries when survival was all-important in a strife-torn countryside. In the following centuries any further introductions were made by the great monasteries, and the cultivation of fruit crops and medicinal herbs was continued by them.

Apart from the Roman period, the introduction of trees, until the sixteenth century, was primarily economic. By the early 1500s the countryside settled down to a more peaceful existence with the coming of the Tudors to the throne. As a result, manor houses no longer needed to be fortified, and houses and gardens were built and developed as the money that former generations had spent on war and defence was now available for more peaceful pursuits. Although the cultivation of flowers and trees continued to be mainly for food and medicinal purposes, it is at about this time that ornamental introductions started to find their way into gardens of

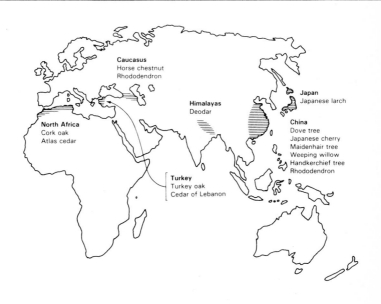

those prosperous enough to own them. It is interesting that many of the trees being grown at this time included species that are also thought to have been grown for the same reasons by the Romans. In a list of trees written in 1548, the sweet bay, Oriental plane, holm oak (evergreen oak), mulberry, stone pine, Italian cypress and Norway spruce are all mentioned, in addition to fruit trees. One newcomer, however, was the lilac which soon became popular as a flowering shrub in gardens designed for visual beauty. In the following century, the number of flowering shrubs and flowers from abroad increased rapidly.

In the sixteenth century, evergreen trees were in demand for formal gardens, as only yew, holly, privet and box were available. Thus, cherry laurel, holm oak, phylleria and Italian cypress began to be used for the geometrical walks that soon became a feature of gardens, providing colour all the year round and some winter protection. It may have also been for this purpose that the first recorded tree from North America was introduced as early as 1596, the white cedar from its east coast.

During the seventeenth century, many collections of trees were started, usually in association with herb gardens and nurseries. One of the most famous collections was that of the Tradescants, father and son, who introduced a large number of new trees from different parts of the world. The elder Tradescant travelled mainly in Europe and had contacts who sent him many specimens for his nursery garden in London. The younger Tradescant travelled to America and many of the early tree introductions from that continent were made by him. Among those familiar today are the false acacia (robinia) and the tulip tree with its striking flowers and foliage.

Another important collector at this time was Bishop Compton who had a garden at Fulham and he appears to have collected for the pleasure it gave him rather than for any material benefit. He had contacts abroad, especially in America and was responsible for the introduction of box elder, balsam poplar, red oak and sweet gum.

At the start of the eighteenth century, the collection and planting of trees was extended considerably by private landowners. With the growth of wealth and the acts of enclosure, more and more people were creating estates in the countryside and laying out their gardens in a less formal manner. For this new landscape, different kinds of trees were sought, both those that could be used in avenues, such as limes and chestnuts, and those to plant as individuals for their beauty or rarity, such as cedars and weeping willows. More people were travelling abroad so that the collection and introduction by many private individuals took place at this time and the number of new trees increased considerably. Many of these were kept under glass in warm conditions initially until it was realised how hardy they really were. During the eighteenth century many specimen trees were imported from the Netherlands which had an established reputation for producing nursery trees.

The beginning of the nineteenth century saw the steady increase in the numbers of new trees. Botanical gardens had been formed and many arboreta were being planted to exhibit the numerous and diverse species available. During this century, the botanic gardens at Kew and Edinburgh, the Royal Horticultural Society and numerous private nurseries (the most well known being that of Veitch) sent collectors to all parts of the world in their search for new trees and plants. William Lobb supplied Veitch with the Wellingtonia and the western red cedar from North America and the monkey-puzzle from South America: this last curiosity became a common feature of Victorian gardens. Wilson, also sent out by Veitch, collected dove tree, many maples and rhododendrons from China. Later, from Japan, he added azaleas and flowering cherries. The most famous collectors employed by the Royal Horticultural Society were Robert Fortune in China, and David Douglas. The latter collected mainly on the west coast of America and introduced a group of trees that were to become very important timber trees here.

The introduction of trees to provide timber had, however, started much earlier with Norway spruce, European larch and European silver fir in the sixteenth and early seventeenth centuries, followed in 1705 by Weymouth pine from America. This marked the beginning of a new influx, that of coniferous timber trees. Gradually these species were planted commercially in increasing quantities by private landowners, perhaps the most famous being the thousands of acres of larch established by successive Dukes of Atholl in Perthshire.

By the end of the nineteenth century, the number of new conifers available had increased considerably, especially those from the north-west coast of America which had a very similar climate. Some of these were introduced by the Oregon Association formed by Scots landowners to collect useful natural products in America. Jeffrey, sent out by them, imported western hemlock and grand fir, first discovered by Douglas. Douglas himself had already introduced Douglas fir, noble fir and Sitka spruce.

New Trees

The wide diversity of tree species throughout the world has arisen as a result, first, of genetic variation and then by some of those variations becoming established in a particular environment to which they are suited. Thus we have many species of oak, spruce and maples, just to take three large groups, that have representatives in widely separated parts of the world. Each group has evolved from a common ancestor but become specialised to suit a particular location. There are oaks in Europe, North America and the Far East, for instance, that occupy sites with similar soil and climatic conditions. The European Norway spruce merges in European Russia with the Siberian spruce to the extent that the two species are indistinguishable in the centre of their joint range but are clearly distinct species at the eastern and western extremities of it. The visitor to the western states of Canada and the United States is surprised to see big-leaf maple occupying exactly similar sites to that occupied by sycamore (also a maple) in Britain.

Although the continents have been separated for a long time, tree species only evolve slowly and species within a genus are often still very similar. When brought together again by man, they may still be close enough genetically for the pollen of one to fertilise the female flower of the other, producing a new tree, usually with characteristics from both parents. There are several cases where this has happened naturally. Damson is thought to be a natural cross between myrobalan plum and sloe, and has been perpetuated for its fruit. There is some doubt whether grey poplar is a true species or a hybrid between aspen from northern Europe and white poplar from southern Europe. The evidence for this is based on the very variable leaf shape, sometimes like aspen and sometimes like white poplar. Perhaps the most well-known and remarkably useful natural hybrid in Britain is London plane which occurred when Oriental plane and American plane were grown together in the famous Lambeth garden of John Tradescant in the middle of the seventeenth century. Whether he intentionally planted the two parents together is not known, but a large seedling is thought to have been sent to the Oxford Botanic Gardens where it was later recognised as a hybrid which fortunately breeds true and from which our present-day London plane is derived. It has proved remarkably suitable for planting in the soot-laden atmosphere of city parks due to its ability to shed large patches of bark, exposing younger bark beneath with breathing pores not yet filled with soot. Before the Clean Air Act in the early 1950s some inner-city areas were too polluted to grow any other species of tree successfully.

The Lucombe oak arose in a similar way to the London plane. Parent trees of Turkey oak and cork oak from the eastern and western Mediterranean were growing in a Mr Lucombe's nursery at Exeter in 1762 and he noticed seedlings with evergreen Turkey oak-like leaves. He realised that they were hybrids and was able to sell them successfully as a new ornamental tree. The familiar red horse chestnut, which is such a suitable avenue tree, is an intentional cross between the white European horse chestnut and the red American buckeye. When this is crossed again with horse chestnut, it retains the red flowers but they are sterile so that the fruits, or 'conkers', are not produced to attract small boys who so often damage chest-nut trees.

European larch had been an important forest and ornamental tree in Britain for some time before Japanese larch was introduced in the middle of last century. Although the native homes of both trees are far apart, the trees are very similar in appearance and it was not

Dunkeld larch

Leyland cypress

long before hybrid seedlings were found in the forest nursery of the Atholl estate in Tayside at Dunkeld. Apparently, cones collected from young avenue trees of Japanese larch contained seed arising from fertilisation by the pollen of some much older European larch growing on a bank above. The resulting hybrid, Dunkeld larch, has proved a better forest tree than either of its parents. Like many hybrids, it is particularly vigorous so that it grows quickly and produces a higher yield of timber. The stem is usually straight like European larch, eliminating the corkscrew twist common in Japanese larch. Resistance to larch canker, which so often makes European larch valueless, has been acquired from the canker-resistant Japanese larch. It is truly a tree that has combined the best of both worlds.

The story of hybrid, or Leyland, cypress is similar but is unusual as the parents are from different, although closely-related, genera. Nootka cypress (a false cypress) from the north-western American seaboard does not occur naturally with Monterey cypress which is confined to the Monterey peninsula of California, but when they were grown close together on an estate in Wales, natural crosses occurred at least twice. This has produced a remarkably vigorous hybrid, with very dense foliage, which grows very much faster than either parent, adding four to six feet (1.2 – 1.8m) in height a year, so that it has become a popular hedging and screening tree.

Some trees are naturally very variable and periodically produce individuals with a new colour or shape. If these are useful or attractive they are perpetuated, usually by cuttings. The most variable tree in both colour and form is Lawson cypress of which there are about 100 named varieties, ranging from green, blue, grey, yellow and variegated leaf colour as well as various shapes from dwarf, spreading rock-garden shrubs to tall, columnar forest trees. Most would have no place in the tree's natural forest home—indeed, it is not particularly variable there—but in gardens it has immense value as an ornamental tree providing variety of colour and shape suitable for many settings. Another example is Atlas cedar which normally has green foliage in its native north African home but European gardeners have perpetuated the occasional tree with blue foliage for ornamental purposes. The wide range of ornamental cherries, both single- and double-flowered, first developed by the Japanese, have also found an important place in our gardens and as street trees.

With the intention of improving timber yields and quality, foresters select seeds from the best trees to sow in nurseries in order to produce improved young trees for the next crop. Straightness of stem, light branching (to reduce knots in the timber), vigorous growth and wood with a straight grain and long fibres, can all be achieved by selection. Such improvements can be further increased by producing seed in 'seed orchards'.

Here, flowering branches from mature trees of good quality are grafted on to young, vigorous root-stocks to produce small trees that will flower heavily at a height that can be reached from the ground. Pollination can then be controlled so that only pollen from the best trees is used and the resulting seed from known good parents can be collected easily. These techniques can increase the yield of timber by at least ten per cent in the first generation and provide young trees suited to particular sites. Foresters no longer talk about planting Scots pine or Sitka spruce; rather, they refer to a particular strain of Scots pine from a known location in Scotland in the same climatic zone as the planting site, or a 'provenance' of Sitka spruce from a similar climate in British Columbia in Canada that is known to do well here.

In all these ways, man is making use of the infinite variety that nature is continually providing, enriching the natural heritage. More trees with greater variety are becoming available all the time. The range of sites for which trees are required has increased to include artificial city and industrial wasteland, so that the present-day treescape is more diverse than ever before.

Perpetuating Our Tree Heritage

The history of the conservation of woodlands is inseparable from the history of conservation as a whole because woodlands provide the habitat for many other forms of wildlife. The study of natural history first became popular in the nineteenth century. The rise in interest was due to a number of social changes, the most significant being the increased leisure time available, especially among the middle classes. Clergymen, in particular, formed a large proportion of the eminent naturalists who emerged during this period. As a result of this rise in popularity, many different societies, devoted to all branches of natural history, came into existence. The inclusion of the words 'field club' in the title of many of these reflected the emphasis on outdoor activities and expeditions into the countryside which had become more accessible with the development of the railways. Such activities required little funding or organisation and kept the cost of joining a club at a reasonable level. Many of the societies still exist today and take a prominent part in conservation.

To begin with, the emphasis was on the collection of specimens, and vast numbers of animals, plants and insects were obtained, not only by people interested in natural history but also by those who indulged in the Victorian craze for collections of all kinds. This led to drastic reductions in the numbers of some species. In addition, birds and animals were also shot for sport or because they interfered with it, and the lists of bird and animal predators destroyed by the big estates at this time make depressing reading. The countryside took many years to recover from the effects of such depredations and some species were lost altogether.

When the realisation of what was happening began to dawn, it became expressed in the formation of bodies whose aim was protection. Out of this movement came the formation, to mention but a few, of the Commons, Open Spaces and Footpaths Preservation Society in 1865, the National Trust in 1895 and the Royal Society for the Protection of Birds (RSPB) in 1889, this last by a small group of ladies who pledged not to wear birds' plumage. As well as organisations for protection, the first attempts at conservation were also emerging. The setting aside of reserves for the protection and conservation of animals had been carried out as early as 1813 by some enlightened landowners but the first co-operative effort was the acquisition of Breydon as a reserve in the Norfolk Broads in 1888, foreshadowing future trends. This led to the formation of the Society for the Promotion of Nature Reserves in 1912.

Attention now began to turn from dead specimens to living ones, and plants and animals began to be studied in their natural surroundings. Cameras, binoculars and notebooks began to take the place of guns and collecting equipment. Huxley's studies on behaviour, Eliot Howard's on bird territories, Tansley's classification of British vegetation types and Elton's animal ecology and population studies were among the major contributions to the new approach. It began to be appreciated that living things were not static and fixed but that they were changing and adapting all the time. These studies led to the science of ecology, so important in understanding the interrelationships between plants and animals. A new form of 'collecting' now began to emerge, that of surveys and distribution records which showed the status of plants, trees, animals and insects and gave an indication of their rarity and changes in numbers. Such surveys continue today and the amateur naturalist makes an important contribution to the process by collecting records in the field.

One survey with wide implications for conservation was the Land Utilisation Survey in 1930 carried out by Dudley Stamp, highlighting the rapid loss of agricultural land. This led to land classification and the idea of planning resources for the future, including the formation of nature reserves. As a result, the Nature Conservancy was formed in 1949 with national funds available for the first time in the field of conservation. The first reserve to be established was Beinn Eighe in Highland which contained a large area of natural Scots pine woodland. In addition to reserves, the acquisition of a number of 'Sites of Special Scientific Interest' (SSSIs) have been designated for some particular species or geological formation so that they would not be inadvertently destroyed or damaged. Some of these include areas of primary woodland which have never been cleared for agricultural purposes. A *Nature Conservation Review*, recently published, lists all sites considered of importance for conservation, those already designated and additional areas considered desirable; about a third of these are woodlands.

With encouragement from the Nature Conservancy, Naturalists' Trusts began to multiply and these purchased and administered nature reserves in their own particular areas. As well as promoting conservation by the establishment of reserves, research began into the study of ecological problems so that the results could be applied to the understanding of plant and animal communities. The handing over to the Nature Conservancy of the records of the plant distribution schemes by the Botanical Society of the British Isles laid the foundation of the Biological Records Centre.

From the establishment of nature reserves, the Nature Conservancy changed to a wider concept of conservation, realising that reserves alone were only part of improving and conserving the environment. From the 'Countryside Conferences' that resulted in the 1960s, the public were made aware of conservation and became more involved in it. In the early 1970s the Nature Conservancy was replaced by two bodies: the Nature Conservancy Council, which became responsible for conservation; and the Natural Environment Research Council, which carries out research, both at its own institutes and at others aided by grants.

Side by side with the Nature Conservancy, after the Second World War the National Parks Commission was established which later became the Countryside Commission. Under the Commission, ten national parks were formed and more recently, 'Areas of Outstanding Natural Beauty' designated, one of the largest of which covers the Chiltern beechwoods. National Parks are administered by the local authority who also have the responsibility for Tree Preservation Orders. Such orders prevent the felling of individual trees or small areas of woodland that have an amenity value. Local authorities can also designate conservation areas in which notice has to be given if any tree is to be felled or lopped. Tree planting is encouraged by grants from the Countryside Commission.

The Forestry Commission, founded in 1919, has become involved in conservation in recent years. Originally set up to develop a national reserve of timber, its activities have now widened into the fields of recreation and conservation, with, for example, research carried out on trees in relation to wildlife. Although, in the past, planting policies may have deserved the criticism levelled at them, this is no longer the case. Conservation and landscaping form an important part of its activities and opening of extensive forest areas for recreational facilities to the public has resulted in educating people about trees and conservation, by means of nature walks, museums and school projects. The Commission also exercises control over tree felling by issuing licences.

As well as Government-financed conservation, a number of important voluntary organisations exist which have made and are making significant contributions. The Society for the Promotion of Nature Reserves took over the task of acting as an 'umbrella' body, advising and assisting individual naturalists' trusts, and in 1958 became the Society for the Promotion of Nature Conservation. The National Trust, established in 1895, had its origin in the opposition to the felling of some fine Scots pine trees on the side of Derwentwater in the Lake District and, together with the National Trust for Scotland, is now the third largest landowner in Britain with many woodland conservation and other environmental interests. The Councils for the Protection of Rural England and Wales seek to protect the environment as a whole, as does the Council for Environmental Conservation (now incorporating the Council for Nature) which seeks to maintain contact and liaison between the numerous natural history societies and to encourage active conservation in all fields. The much more recently formed Tree Council seeks to draw together organisations interested in the amenity value of trees and the enhancement of the country's treescape.

The way conservation is to move in the future needs to be carefully planned. Already the trend towards co-operation between various bodies is there and this will need to be developed into further co-ordinated efforts. It has been evident for some time that natural history should be regarded as a whole, an intricate pattern of species interlocking and working with each other. Regarded in this light it is logical that conservation areas should be for whole ecosystems rather than for individual species and co-operation should develop between all interested bodies. Reserves should be managed jointly to make sure that the right ecological balance is kept to conserve the whole ecosystem. This will help to spread limited finances rather than when each society jealously guards its own interests for one purpose only. In the same way, multi-use of land will allow the maximum use to be made of its potential. Forests open to the public have already led the way in this field.

Priorities for conservation need to be decided between various organisations in order to make the best use of resources. It is probably a waste to spend money endeavouring to preserve a species when major natural changes, such as climate, may be the overall controlling factor. Extinction of some species and favouring of others have occurred since life appeared on the earth and, once numbers fall to a critically low level, the battle is lost. Such a species may best be perpetuated artificially in zoos, botanic gardens or as seed in gene banks, thus preserved for re-introduction when conditions are suitable. There may be little point in spending money to preserve a species that is common elsewhere, especially within the British Isles. International co-operation is also becoming important to preserve species only occurring in particular countries, to extend protection to migrating insects and birds and to prevent the spread of diseases to trees and plants. International co-operation in conservation is of great importance and the promotion, in 1980, of a World Conservation Strategy is a major step in this direction.

Hand in hand with conservation, there now emerges the challenge of perpetuation. Trees fall into various categories requiring different methods of management. There are the remnants of the pioneers scattered over the British Isles which, because of their age, contain unique ecosystems. These communities cannot be replaced by merely stepping up the planting of native trees in other areas. They require detailed study of the factors that maintain them in equilibrium and planned management to ensure regeneration, so that the forest community continues to perpetuate.

Many of these woodlands are in private hands and have only survived because they have been part of integrated estates and farmland. In some cases, broad-minded owners, if given financial assistance, would wish to perpetuate these woods for the benefit of future generations. There is scope, too, in persuading farmers and landowners to leave parts of farms that are not easily cultivated, as amenity woodland and to plant unused areas with trees. Small blocks of woodlands have been shown to be much more useful as a wildlife reserve than hedges.

One of the greatest pitfalls that many people, intent on preserving trees, fall into is to forget that trees are living and will not remain unchanged but will live and die like everything else. This is especially evident with some tree preservation orders which seek to preserve senile trees. In addition, conservation for trees has so far been concentrated on broadleafed woodland remnants, but forest plantations are now beginning to develop into integrated ecosystems and, given time, will be important to wildlife conservation. Although it is often advocated that native trees should be planted to increase wildlife, research is beginning to show that plantations also contribute significantly. Evidence is accumulating that, for many species of plants, animals and birds, it does not matter whether the tree species is hardwood or conifer, native or not. Studies comparing bird populations in Scots pine and Corsican pine plantations have shown no significant differences in the number of species at equivalent ages, the diversity of species in both increasing with the age of the plantation. It is also evident from this study that the morphology (that is, the shape and form) of the tree is more important than whether it is an exotic or not. Studies of vegetation in coniferous plantations show that, except under very dense spruce, most plants that would be found in hardwoods in the same area are also present and these are quick to re-invade any openings in the canopy. Plantations of young, dense broadleafed woods are as low in diversity of bird species as conifers, contrary to the popular view that planting broadleafed trees automatically increases wildlife.

As a wood ages, species diversity increases whether conifer or broadleafed, though the latter may support a higher density. The number of species in a wood is further increased by other factors such as roads, unplanted areas, streams and, once the forest is mature enough, by felled areas. Future forestry will not be so uniform and will thus provide a range of diverse habitats. Some species of birds and bats can be increased by the provision of artificial nesting boxes and roosting sites, the lack of these often being a limitation in young woodland. Birds can also be encouraged in plantations by leaving some older trees which will provide such sites and also conserve insect species.

It can be seen, therefore, that there are two main tasks ahead in the perpetuation of our tree heritage and the species in balance with it. One is to maintain the remnants of the pioneers and the unique associations that have evolved with them. This needs careful study and selective manipulation to keep what is required within the constraints of climate and other factors. Secondly, afforestation must be increased for economic reasons but this will also, in many ways, be an advantage to our wildlife heritage. It has already encouraged increases in wildlife by providing protection for animals, flowers, insects, plants and, particularly, birds. As the forests mature, suitable habitats will attract further invasions.

As well as woodlands, individual trees also require looking after. These also have finite lifespans and, if the environment is to be planned carefully, younger trees need to be planted long before any signs of decay appear. The growing of some rare species will also act as a reserve for trees at the verge of extinction in their native habitat. Already the handkerchief tree, lost in its native home, has been returned to China from Britain.

Aboreta and Tree Collections

An arboretum is a collection of all types of specimen trees, while a 'pinetum' includes all conifers, not just pines. There are a large number of both throughout this country. Most of them were started by enthusiastic individuals but many are now in public ownership or belong to the National Trust and the National Trust for Scotland. The large majority can be visited by the general public, either all the year round or on open days. In addition, there are a few experimental areas where small plots of exotic species are being tested under woodland conditions. These are called forest gardens or forest plots. They are all well worth a visit by anyone interested in trees. The map opposite shows the location of some of the more notable tree collections and each is briefly described. The owners are named in brackets.

1 **Inverewe,** Highland (National Trust for Scotland).
A unique colection of tender trees on a mild but wind-swept coast.

2 **Diana's Grove,** Atholl Estates, Tayside (Duke of Atholl).
A collection of north-western American trees showing growth to remarkable heights, as well as one of the original hybrid larches.

3 **Scone Palace,** Perth, Tayside (The Earl of Mansfield).
Many fine conifers from mid-nineteenth-century introductions, including the first Douglas fir grown in Britain.

4a **Royal Botanic Gardens,** Edinburgh and
& b **Younger Botanic Gardens,** Benmore, Strathclyde (Department of the Environment).
A very wide collection of evergreen and deciduous trees from all parts of the world at Edinburgh, and large conifers in the milder climate of the subsidiary Benmore gardens.

5 **Crarae,** Inveraray, Strathclyde (Forestry Commission).
Many rare trees and forest plots of rare conifers.

6 **Kilmun Forest Garden,** Benmore, Strathclyde (Forestry Commission).
Trial plots of many conifers.

7 **Castlewellan,** County Down, Northern Ireland (Forest Service).
A large collection of trees, many of great size, including some tender species.

8 **Studley Royal,** Ripon, North Yorkshire (North Yorkshire County Council).
Large oaks, sweet chestnuts and other trees.

9 **Granada Arboretum,** Nantwich, Cheshire (Manchester University).
A recent collection with a wide range of trees.

10 **Glasnevin Botanic Garden,** Dublin, Eire.
Many fine and rare trees.

11 **Powerscourt,** Wicklow, Eire.
A large collection of vigorously growing conifers.

12 **Bodnant,** Conway, Gwynedd (National Trust).
A garden rather than a tree collection but including some very fine trees.

13 **Vivod Forest Garden,** Llangollen, Clwyd (Forestry Commission).
Individual trees and a wide range of conifer forest plots at a high elevation planted in the last 30 years.

14 **Naylor Pinetum and Redwood Grove,** Leighton, Welshpool, Powys (Royal Forestry Society of England, Wales and Northern Ireland).
Thirty-three large coast redwoods originally brought from America over 100 years ago in pots, and a small collection of other conifers.

15 **Cambridge Botanic Gardens,** Cambridge (Cambridge University).
A wide collection of deciduous trees, including many unusual species.

16 **Oxford Botanic Gardens and University Parks,** Oxford (Oxford University).

Rare old trees and, in the Parks, many fine deciduous specimens.

17 Batsford Park, Moreton-in-Marsh, Gloucestershire (Lord Dulverton).
A varied collection including some unusual oaks.

18 Westonbirt Arboretum, Tetbury, Gloucestershire (Forestry Commission).
A very large collection of all types of temperate trees.

19 Queenswood, Hope under Dinmore, Hereford and Worcester (Hereford and Worcester County Council).
An old woodland area traversed by the A49 road and now open to the public. Many specimen trees have been planted in recent years.

20 Speech House, Coleford, Gloucestershire (Forestry Commission).
Unusual trees, mainly conifers, some recently planted.

21 Cardiff Parks, South Glamorgan (Cardiff City Council).
Many interesting trees, particularly in Roath Park and Cefn On Park.

22 Dyffryn House, Mid-Glamorgan (Glamorgan County Council).
A varied collection of flowering trees and shrubs.

23 London Parks (Department of the Environment).
Interesting trees in Hyde Park, Kensington Gardens, St James's Park and Regent's Park; magnificent London planes in Green Park and elsewhere.

24 Syon House, Brentford, London (Duke of Northumberland).
A very old and extensive collection.

25a Royal Botanic Gardens, Kew, Richmond,
& b Surrey and **Wakehurst Place,** Ardingly, West Sussex (Department of the Environment).
Classified collections of all temperate genera that include trees. The arboretum at Kew contains most hardy woody species grouped botanically. Better growing conditions at Wakehurst Place allow a wide collection of fine trees.

26 Hampton Court and **Bushy Park,** London
(Department of the Environment).
Many large old trees and formal avenues. Successional planting carried out in the last 15 years to replace ageing trees.

27 Windsor Great Park, Savill and Valley Gardens, Berkshire (HM the Queen).
Very varied collections, some recently planted.

28 Wisley Gardens, Ripley, Surrey (Royal Horticultural Society).
Some excellent conifers in the pinetum and many other trees in the gardens.

29 National Pinetum, Bedgebury, Kent (Forestry Commission).
As a pinetum, it includes all hardy conifers as well as over 100 conifer forest plots.

30 Sheffield Park, Uckfield, East Sussex (National Trust).
Many very fine conifers and other trees.

31 Borde Hill, Haywards Heath, West Sussex.
Rare trees, including some fine maples, oaks and various conifers.

32 Nymans, Handcross, West Sussex (National Trust).
A collection of fine conifers and other trees.

33 Exbury, Beaulieu, Hampshire (E. de Rothschild, Esq.).
Many large and some rare trees.

34 Hillier Arboretum, Romsey, Hampshire (Hampshire County Council).
A random collection of young trees, including many rarities and cultivars.

35 Stourhead, Mere, Wiltshire (National Trust).
A varied collection of mature trees.

36 Bicton, Sidmouth, Devon (Lord Clinton).
A wide range of very fine trees in the gardens and pinetum.

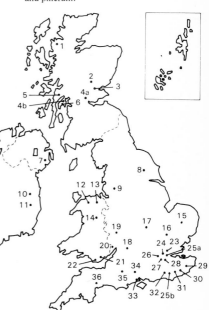

Tree Societies

There are several societies whose members are interested in trees and woodland, and anyone interested in trees can join them, whether academically qualified or not. Their mixed memberships provide an excellent opportunity for the exchange of ideas between the professional and enthusiastic amateur which is of benefit to both. They all publish journals and arrange outdoor and indoor meetings for their members. They have also done a great deal to foster the conservation of our tree heritage.

These societies range through forestry and aboriculture; most have an interest in both. Forestry is the scientific management of woodlands and plantations primarily for the production of timber and other wood products. A forester, therefore, is concerned with the interrelationship between trees as they grow together in a woodland. Arboriculture, on the other hand, is concerned with the amenity value of trees and an arboriculturist finds himself more often looking after individual trees than whole woodlands.

The Royal Scottish Forestry Society
16 Abercomby Place, Edinburgh EH3 6LB
There has always been a particularly strong interest in forestry and trees in Scotland, and it is for this reason that the Royal Scottish Forestry Society is the oldest in Britain. It was formed in 1854 as the Scottish Arboricultural Society and has always been active in furthering the interests of forestry and foresters. It publishes *Scottish Forestry* and has an interest in forestry education, until recently offering its own examinations.

The Royal Forestry Society of England, Wales and Northern Ireland
102 High Street, Tring, Hertfordshire HP23 4AH
This was founded as the English Arboricultural Society and will celebrate its centenary in 1982. It is much the largest of the various tree societies. It has a similar role to the Royal Scottish Forestry Society but has a more active interest in arboriculture in which it offers a professional examination, the National Diploma in Arboriculture. It also owns a unique stand of coast redwoods and a small pinetum in Wales (no. 14 in the previous chapter). The *Quarterly Journal of*

Forestry, which it publishes, includes both forestry and arboricultural articles.

Neither of the royal societies have a royal charter. They are not professional institutes but they have royal patronage.

The Arboricultural Association
Dunkirk Farm, Southwick, Trowbridge, Wiltshire
This is a more recent body and to some extent a professional body for practising aboriculturists, but it also has lay members. It publishes the *Arboricultural Journal*.

The Men of Trees
Crawley Down, Crawley, West Sussex
This society was founded in 1922 and is an international society with a wholly amateur membership of men and women with an enthusiastic interest in trees, particularly tree planting on a world scale. Their journal is *Trees*.

The Woodland Trust
Ivybridge, Devon PL21 0JQ
This was formed in 1972 to conserve ancient broadleafed woodlands and establish new ones. It purchases or accepts gifts of woodlands which are managed to encourage all forms of wildlife with as little interference as possible. Most of their present woods are in the south of England, particularly Devon. The Trust publishes a list of its woodlands for members and some are open to the public.

Anyone interested in trees and wanting to know more about them will benefit from joining one or more of these tree societies. A great deal can be learnt in an informal way from their meetings and from the articles in their journals.

How a Tree Grows

Plants of almost all forms, including trees, have not achieved the powers of movement as animals have, and must remain stationary. As they are dependent on light for the fundamental process of photosynthesis by which they synthesise food in their green parts, there is intense competition to reach the light and avoid shade cast by other vegetation. Most plants, therefore, grow upwards and trees are the plants that have exploited this characteristic to the full by growing well above and dominating all other forms of vegetation.

Some trees achieve very great heights, such as Douglas fir and western red cedar on the north-west Pacific coast of America, reaching 300 feet (91.5 m) and more. Here, too, are found the tallest trees in the world, the coast redwoods, many of which are over 350 feet (107 m). In Britain trees do not grow as tall as this because conditions here are not as suitable, being both windy and exposed. However, some Douglas fir trees here are already over 170 feet (52m) high although the tree has only been in this country for 150 years. As they are still growing, heights in excess of 200 feet (61 m) are likely to be achieved eventually, not only by Douglas fir but also by some of the other exotic conifers that grow so well here.

Trees have been able to perfect this achievement of obtaining height, and thus dominance, over other plants by the production of woody tissues. The cell walls in the stem are thickened with lignin, a stiffening material, which provides them with great strength and durability, both of which are important characteristics. The pressure on the crown of a large tree in a gale, at the top of a long trunk which acts as a lever, is very considerable. The very long life of trees, several hundreds of years for some of our native trees and several thousands of years for some of the north-west American conifers, gives them time to grow to these great heights. This ability is gained not only by upward growth but also by the addition of a new layer of woody tissue under the bark each year so that the tree is constantly expanding in diameter. The vital ring of living cells that produces this new layer annually is just under the bark, and if this is severely damaged the tree will suffer or even die.

In the temperate climate of Britain, with its marked contrast between summer and winter, growth mainly takes place in the summer. When a tree is felled, the annual rings of growth can be seen on the butt and cut stump. This is because the ring of new wood added in the spring is composed of cells with large spaces in their centre surrounded by lignified walls. A function of the woody tissue is to provide a series of 'pipes' for conducting water drawn from the soil up to the leaves. Later in the summer, growth slows down, not so much water is needed and very thick-walled cells are produced, mainly to provide strength. These thicker-walled cells are darker in colour and contrast with the springwood cells so that an annual ring can be seen.

Annual rings

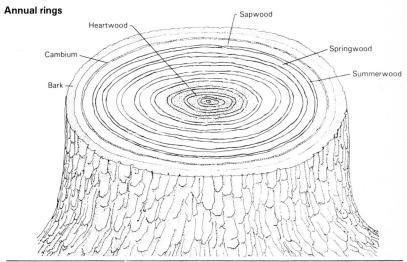

How a tree makes food

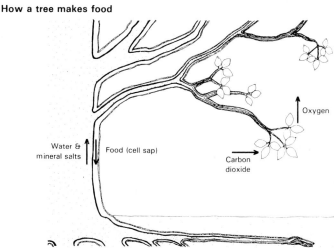

A 'sleeve' of woody tissue with hollow cells on the inside (springwood) and thick-walled cells (summerwood) on the outside is thus added under the bark each year. This 'sleeve' encloses the branches and twigs as well as the main stem. At the base of the trunk there will be a ring representing every year since the tree was planted or grew from a natural seedling, but in the branches there will only be rings for the years since the branch first developed. At the top of the tree, therefore, there will be fewer annual rings but everywhere on the tree the outside ring is the most recently formed and, therefore, the youngest.

As a tree increases in size it ceases to use the innermost rings for water conduction but, due to its greater size, it does need them to provide strength. After about 20 to 40 years, therefore, varying from one tree species to another, the innermost conducting cells die and their empty tube-like centres become blocked up to provide added strength. Thus the centre of the trunk becomes non-living material of great strength providing an upright 'spar' to support the ever-increasing crown up in the sunlight where it can function best. This dead 'heartwood' in the centre of the tree becomes darker than the living 'sapwood' surrounding it, although the distinction between the light-coloured springwood cells and the darker-coloured summerwood cells can still be seen within it. This strong, dead and durable heartwood has many structural uses as timber when the tree is eventually cut down.

The leaves of trees are raised up into the sunlight so that they can carry out the process of photosynthesis—which is fundamental to all life, both plant and animal—as efficiently as possible. The green pigment in the leaves combines carbon dioxide from the air with minerals brought up from the soil through the roots and then the sapwood of the stem, branches and twigs. Sugars are formed which are later synthesised into more complex foods and, in the process, energy is stored, while oxygen is released into the atmosphere. This unique process can only be carried out by the green pigment called chlorophyll which is possessed by green plants. When the food is used later by the tree, or eaten further on in the 'food chain' by animals, the stored energy is released by a process, similar to burning, during which oxygen is added.

When the food has been formed in the leaf, it is transferred, in solution, in the form of cell sap back down the stem of the tree to be stored for future use. The sap flows through thin-walled cells just under the bark. These also develop from the same growth cells that produce the woody cells of the stem but are outside them, forming similar 'sleeve' over the whole tree. They are protected by the corky bark but, if this is removed in a ring right round the tree, or even constricted by a tie supporting a young planted tree, the downward movement of the food supply is interrupted and the tree will soon die.

Leaves are fragile structures composed of thin-walled cells to allow the exchange of carbon dioxide and oxygen through their surfaces and yet they are subject to a lot of desiccation and buffeting by wind. They have, therefore, found two means of protecting themselves and reducing water loss. Evergreen trees have small, thick, usually needle-like leaves that can survive winter for a few years before falling. Deciduous trees, which are mainly the more advanced broadleafed trees, have leaves that only last one summer and make optimum use of the best time of the year. Their large, soft leaves usually have long stalks, are cleverly arranged in mosaics to catch the maximum amount of sunlight and fall in the autumn so as to avoid the rigours of winter.

Having achieved great height for the purpose of reaching the light and a durable stem lasting many years, trees need not flower early in life or every year. They also have the advantage of dispersing their seeds from great heights so that many of these are wind-borne. Their flowers usually develop high up in the crown so that they get the maximum amount of sunlight to ripen. Many trees only produce large quantities of seed periodically in good 'seed years' when climatic conditions have allowed the accumulation of abundant food reserves the year before. These reserves are then available in the early spring when the flowers are produced, thus leaving the whole summer for ripening the seeds.

The flowers and fruits of broadleafed trees are generally more conspicuous than those of conifers as they are often pollinated by insects and the seeds are dispersed by animals. Conifers have small flowers which are often red or yellow, high up in the crowns. These develop later in the season into woody cones containing many winged seeds which are dispersed by air currents.

How to Identify Trees

Botanical classification is based on flowers because groups of trees that have similar flowers have evolved from a common ancestor. However, as trees do not flower early in life and their flowers are often inaccessible high up in the tree, practical identification is usually based on the leaves. There are snags in this because some unrelated trees have leaves that are alike, such as wild service tree which is often taken for a maple, so other factors are useful for confirmation, such as bark, twig colour, buds and the shape of the tree.

The first thing to do, however, is to look at the leaves and note two things about them. Are they 'simple' leaves with just a single leaf blade, such as cherry, or are they 'compound' leaves with many leaflets either side of an extended leaf stalk, such as ash? If they are simple leaves they may be triangular like birch, lobed like oak or deeply divided like sycamore. If they are compound, the leaflets may be in a hand-shaped arrangement, called 'palmate', such as horse chestnut. Many leaves have toothed margins and some are identified by the shape of the leaf base which may be rounded, flat, unequal on each side, heart-shaped or 'auricled' (ear-like).

While leaf shape can vary considerably, the arrangement of leaves on the twigs of all broadleafed trees falls quite distinctly into one of two categories. They are either 'alternate' or 'opposite'. Leaves arranged alternately occur on the stem first on one side and then a little further up on the other side, the third leaf on the same side as the first and so on. Oppositely arranged leaves occur in pairs opposite each other and each pair is at right angles to the pair above it and the one below it. Careful observation of the leaf arrangement will put a tree firmly into one group and exclude it from the other and so it is a key factor to look for. One of our less common native trees, the wild service tree, is often taken for a maple because its leaves are very like the maple's. In fact it is a *Sorbus*, like rowan and whitebeam which have compound and simple leaves respectively. The important thing to note is that the wild service tree has alternate leaves, whereas maples have opposite leaves. Leaf arrangement then is a reliable character for identification while leaf shape is only a guide.

Most broadleafed trees that grow in Britain drop their leaves in winter, and so for nearly half the year these are not available for identification. However, the buds are present instead, because they form towards the end of the summer and remain dormant over the winter, ready to develop new leaves immediately the spring weather is suitable. Thus they are available for identification all through the winter and, while their colour and shape are characteristic and are a useful guide, their arrangement is the most reliable identifying feature. This is because they were formed during the summer in the axils of the leaves, that is, just above the leaf stalk and between it and the stem. When the leaves fall, the buds show the former positions of the leaves and are themselves either alternately or oppositely arranged.

In both winter and summer, trees can be recognised in a general way and, with some experience, by the shape of their crowns. Some are rounded like oak or spreading like horse chestnut, while others are narrow like Lombardy (but not other) poplars. Branches, too, more easily seen in the winter, are characteristic: on English oak they

Leaf shapes

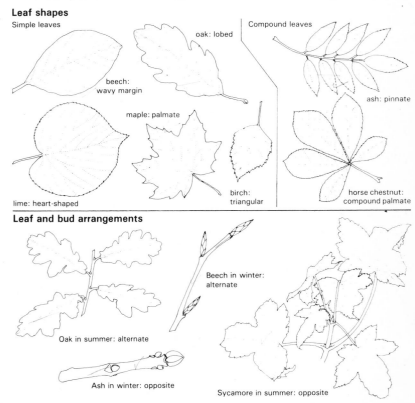

Simple leaves

oak: lobed

Compound leaves

beech: wavy margin

ash: pinnate

maple: palmate

lime: heart-shaped

birch: triangular

horse chestnut: compound palmate

Leaf and bud arrangements

Oak in summer: alternate

Beech in winter: alternate

Ash in winter: opposite

Sycamore in summer: opposite

are generally horizontal, while on sessile oak they tend to rise upwards. Lime has arching branches and Norway spruce has descending branches, while those of silver fir are level. In 'A Selection of Species', an outline has been drawn for each species of tree described, showing both summer and winter profiles where applicable, and these are an aid to identifying trees at a distance but they need to be confirmed by looking at the leaves, twigs or, sometimes, the bark.

The bark pattern is similar for all the trees of one species. It is, however, difficult to describe in words and identification is learned by experience. Some bark is very characteristic. Sweet chestnut, for instance, has long furrows which are usually twisted to the right or left; the twist becomes more pronounced as the tree ages. The bark of Scots pine is red in the crown of the tree while on other pines it is dark coloured. Wild cherry bark peels off in horizontal strips and birch bark is white and papery. Bark tends to change with the age of the tree. On young trees it is smooth and often light coloured but, as the tree ages, it gets furrowed and darker. The furrowing occurs because the tree increases in diameter as it grows and the bark has to split to allow for this. It does not split right down to the living tissue below and, indeed, more bark is being added on the inside all the time. The splitting occurs in different ways, resulting in patterns characteristic of each species of tree. Perhaps the most characteristic bark of all is that of the London plane which scales off to leave large, light-coloured patches of the living under-bark showing.

Fruit and seeds of many species remain on the tree for at least the early part of the winter and are an accurate aid to identification at a time when this is difficult. The single 'keys' of ash remain in clusters for many months and the double 'keys' of sycamore can be seen for some weeks after the leaves have fallen. Horse chestnuts, sweet chestnuts, acorns and beechnuts fall early but can often be found under the parent trees as a guide to their identification. When cones can be seen on or found below conifers, they are often an easier means of identification than the evergreen needles that many beginners find difficulty in recognising.

Flowers, too, help in identification; for instance, in early spring, hazel is characterised by its long, yellow male catkins and tiny, forked scarlet female flowers. The former are often known as 'lamb's tails'. The large, grey and rather fluffy female catkins of goat willow and other sallows are well known and give the trees the name of 'pussy willow' and make them easy to identify before the leaves emerge.

A Selection of Species

Fifty of the most common species in Britain have been chosen for illustration and description in this book. These include some that are known to be native and some others that have been here a long time, as well as a small selection of the many introduced trees which are either used for forestry or for amenity purposes. Closely related and similar species are briefly mentioned and the feature which most easily distinguishes them is illustrated.

Maps showing past and present distribution have been included, indicating where the trees are most likely to be seen and how they have increased or declined since the ice ages. Man has greatly modified the tree cover by agricultural clearance, by settlement and by planting for both commercial and amenity purposes. The maps are not definitive; they are only a guide to where the trees are thought to have been in the past and where they are most common now, either naturally or due to planting. For recent introductions it is possible to indicate where the tree was first planted in a few individual cases. No indication of density of tree cover or numbers of trees is shown. In many cases, the total number has been greatly reduced by man's activities but they are still common and so no change has been indicated on the map.

The trees described fall into four groups. Firstly, there are the native species that have not shown any change in their geographical range, such as birch, holly, alder, wild cherry, hawthorn, wych elm, oak and Scots pine. Secondly, there are the trees thought to be early introductions but which have been in Britain a long time. They include walnut, sweet chestnut, sycamore, common lime and Norway spruce. The third group are native species whose geographical range has been increased by planting and, in its wake, have sometimes become naturalised. They are mountain ash, whitebeam, bird cherry, black poplar, beech and hornbeam. Finally, there is a large group of trees introduced comparatively recently which are well documented. All have increased substantially. Only a few are described in this book, including some from Europe and Asia.

To use the maps

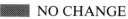

PAST distribution   NO CHANGE

PRESENT distribution   •   introductions to specific sites

Scots Pine

Pinus sylvestris

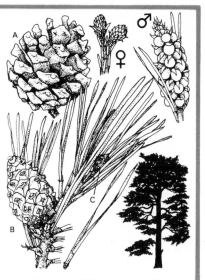

Leaves: needle-like, blue-green, paired, thick, short, sometimes twisted, 2-3 in (5-8 cm); 4-6 in (10-15 cm) on young trees.

Bark: red in the upper part of tree. Flaking in plates. Grey and furrowed at the base.

Buds: small and pointed, ½ in (1 cm).

Flowers: males are yellow, in dense clusters at base of young shoots. Females red, 2-4 at tips of young shoots.

Cones: take 2½ years to mature. Green first year, becoming brown and mature second year. Hang down, pointed; 3 in (8 cm).

Shape: young trees conical, developing flat crown and long clean trunk with age.

A-Mature cone. B-First-year cone. C-Bud.

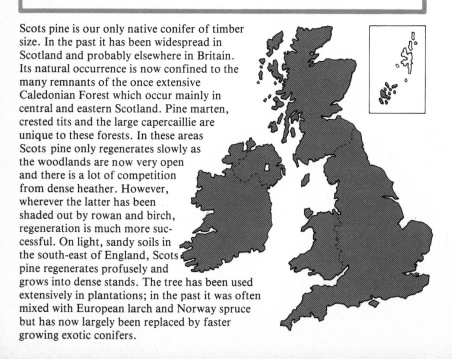

Scots pine is our only native conifer of timber size. In the past it has been widespread in Scotland and probably elsewhere in Britain. Its natural occurrence is now confined to the many remnants of the once extensive Caledonian Forest which occur mainly in central and eastern Scotland. Pine marten, crested tits and the large capercaillie are unique to these forests. In these areas Scots pine only regenerates slowly as the woodlands are now very open and there is a lot of competition from dense heather. However, wherever the latter has been shaded out by rowan and birch, regeneration is much more successful. On light, sandy soils in the south-east of England, Scots pine regenerates profusely and grows into dense stands. The tree has been used extensively in plantations; in the past it was often mixed with European larch and Norway spruce but has now largely been replaced by faster growing exotic conifers.

Shore Pine

Pinus contorta

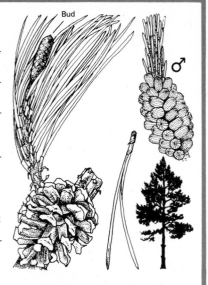

Leaves: needle-like, yellow-green, in pairs. Dense and greener on young trees, often twisted; 1½ - 2 in (3 - 5 cm).

Bark: smooth, greenish-brown and scaly, breaking into corky squares.

Buds: dark brown, bullet-shaped. Sticky with white resin. ½ in (1 cm).

Flowers: male yellow, in dense clusters at base of young shoots. Female red, usually 2-4 at tip of young shoots.

Cones: in whorls of 2-4. Cone scales have prickles. Take 2½ years to mature. Green first year, becoming brown and mature second year. Remain on tree for many years hanging downwards. 2 in (5 cm).

Shape: narrow and tall, with rather bushy foliage.

Originally introduced for its arboricultural value from the north-western seaboard of America in 1855 where it grows in exposed situations, shore pine has become an important plantation tree in this country during the last 50 years. With afforestation of extensive upland areas, it has proved the most successful, and sometimes the only, tree that will grow on the most infertile, wettest and exposed sites. Thus, in north-west Scotland, south-west Scotland, parts of Wales and throughout Ireland, it can now be found growing extensively and coping with the worst conditions. Improved ploughing, draining and fertilising techniques, however, now allow more exacting and valuable species than the shore pine to be grown on all but the poorest sites and the use of shore pine is declining.

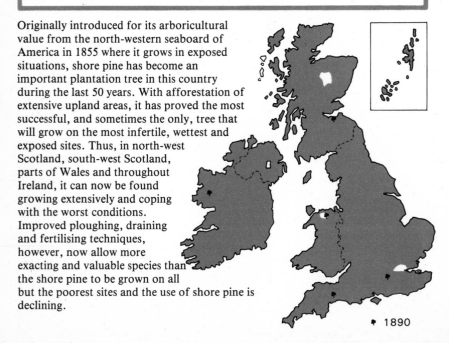

1890

Corsican Pine

Pinus nigra var. *maritima*

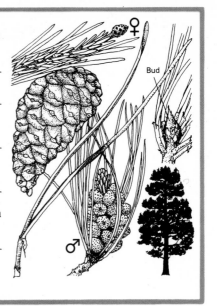

Leaves: needle-like. Dark green, in pairs, long, slender. Shoot brown, feels rough due to the persistant leaf bases after leaves are shed. 4-6in (10-15cm).

Bark: pale grey, becoming dark, cracking into regular plates.

Buds: onion-shaped, brown but often covered with white resin, large; ½-1in (1.2-2.5cm).

Flowers: males yellow, in dense heads at base of shoot. Females pink, at tips of shoot.

Cones: large, rounded, greenish-brown in first year, becoming yellowish-brown when ripe in autumn of second year; 2-3in (5-8cm).

Shape: a tall, dark tree with branches in regular whorls.

Corsican pine is the most suitable variety in this country of the widely distributed black pine of Europe and has been growing here successfully since 1759. It is at home in the drier south and east of Britain but only grows well at low elevations and does not ripen seed in the far north. As a large and vigorous tree able to withstand salt winds, it has been used extensively to provide shelter, particularly on the coast. The rounded, bushy and rather dark-coloured crown is often the backdrop to more sensitive and colourful trees in gardens. It is the most useful timber species that we have for our drier areas. As it grows more quickly and gets a good deal larger than our native Scots pine, it has largely replaced that species in the younger plantations in the south and east of England, although its timber is not quite so strong. It is fortunate that Corsican pine is proving attractive to wildlife.

1800

Norway Spruce

Picea abies

Leaves: needle-like, short, prickly, green, parted below to show light brown shoot. On pegs which remain after leaf has fallen.
½ - 1 in (1.2 - 2.5 cm).

Bark: smooth, light brown, cracking into small plates as the tree ages.

Buds: small and dark brown; ¼ in (6 mm).

Flowers: males yellow, at ends of shoots. Females red, on branches near top of tree.

Cones: cigar-shaped, hanging down; green at first, turning light brown when ripe. Scales have rounded ends. 4 - 6 in (10 - 15 cm).

Shape: triangular, with regular branches.

A-Needle on 'peg'. B-Bud.

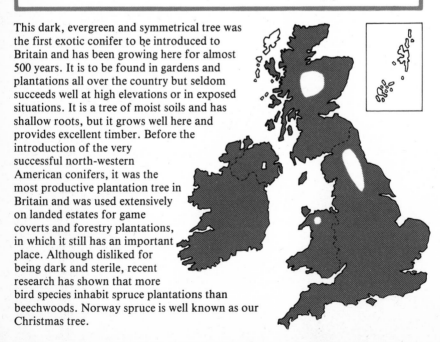

This dark, evergreen and symmetrical tree was the first exotic conifer to be introduced to Britain and has been growing here for almost 500 years. It is to be found in gardens and plantations all over the country but seldom succeeds well at high elevations or in exposed situations. It is a tree of moist soils and has shallow roots, but it grows well here and provides excellent timber. Before the introduction of the very successful north-western American conifers, it was the most productive plantation tree in Britain and was used extensively on landed estates for game coverts and forestry plantations, in which it still has an important place. Although disliked for being dark and sterile, recent research has shown that more bird species inhabit spruce plantations than beechwoods. Norway spruce is well known as our Christmas tree.

Sitka Spruce

Picea sitchensis

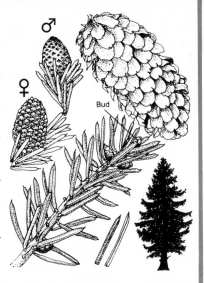

Leaves: needle-like, long, thin and sharp. Green above, bluish bands underneath. Parted below to show pale brown shoot. On pegs which remain when leaf falls. ¾ - 1½ in (2-3 cm).

Bark: grey, smooth, flaking into thin plates.

Buds: small, round, light brown. ¼ in (6 mm).

Flowers: males yellow, at ends of shoots. Females pink, on branches near top of tree.

Cones: lozenge-shaped, hanging down. Green at first, becoming light brown when ripe. Thin, crinkled papery scales have toothed edges. 2-4 in (5-10 cm).

Shape: conical with regular, fine branches.

Bud

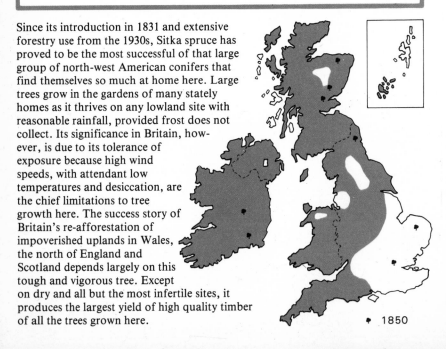

Since its introduction in 1831 and extensive forestry use from the 1930s, Sitka spruce has proved to be the most successful of that large group of north-west American conifers that find themselves so much at home here. Large trees grow in the gardens of many stately homes as it thrives on any lowland site with reasonable rainfall, provided frost does not collect. Its significance in Britain, however, is due to its tolerance of exposure because high wind speeds, with attendant low temperatures and desiccation, are the chief limitations to tree growth here. The success story of Britain's re-afforestation of impoverished uplands in Wales, the north of England and Scotland depends largely on this tough and vigorous tree. Except on dry and all but the most infertile sites, it produces the largest yield of high quality timber of all the trees grown here.

1850

European Larch

Larix decidua

Leaves: pale green soft needles. Single on long shoots, rosettes on short shoots, fall in winter. Twigs straw coloured. ½ - 1½ in (1 - 3 cm).

Bark: grey or light brown, breaking into regular plates with age.

Buds: brown, round, small: ¼ in (6 mm).

Flowers: males yellow, globular, often on underside of shoot as well as above. Females loganberry red with green stripes, erect on shoot.

Cones: egg-shaped, persist for some years after seed is shed. Scales tight. 1 - 1½ in (2.5 - 3 cm).

Shape: conical with fine, descending branches.

Japanese larch *(Larix kaempferi)* differs: blue-green leaves; cone scales turned back; orange twigs.

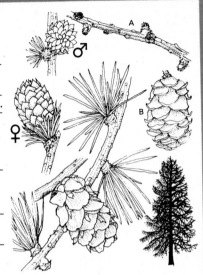

A-Japanese larch twig. B-Japanese larch cone.

European larch has been growing in Britain since early in the 17th century and there are many large, old trees in most parts of the country. It grows well in the drier east but is less healthy in the wetter west, while in frosty areas it is subject to disfiguring stem canker which reduces its rate of growth. European larch has been used extensively for game coverts because it casts a light shade which encourages ground cover. The very similar Japanese larch was introduced in 1861 and soon proved to be a more vigorous tree and much more suited to our climate. It does not suffer from canker and so has become a useful timber tree here. A natural hybrid between the two larches was first noticed at Dunkeld in Perthshire in 1904 but it is likely that hybrid seedlings had been occurring there since 1897. Hybrid larch is even more vigorous than its Japanese parent.

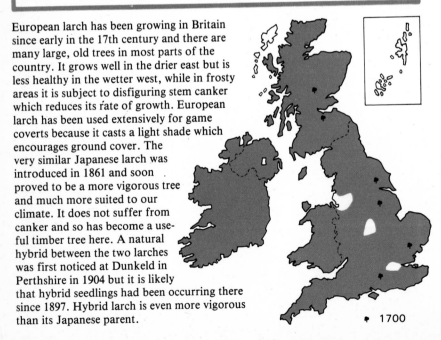

1700

Grand Fir

Abies grandis

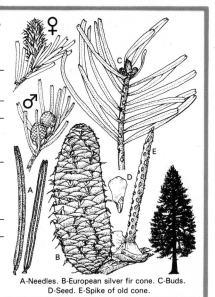

Leaves: flat needles, dark green, shiny, silver below, of different lengths. Flattened to either side of shoot. 1-2 in (2.5-5 cm).

Bark: smooth, grey-green with resin blisters.

Buds: small, purple, resinous. 2 mm.

Flowers: males purple, globular, beneath shoots. Females small, green, cone-shaped, upright.

Cones: cylindrical, bracts hidden. Green, becoming brown when ripe. Remain erect; scales break up to leave central spike. 2-4 in (5-10 cm).

Shape: narrow crown, level branches.

European silver fir *(Abies alba)* differs: sparser foliage; cones larger with bracts showing.

A-Needles. B-European silver fir cone. C-Buds. D-Seed. E-Spike of old cone.

Grand fir was introduced from the west coast of North America in 1832. There are many large grand firs in 'policy woods' around mansion houses, particularly in Scotland, but it is a tree that does not like exposure and seldom succeeds at high altitudes. Under plantation conditions in sheltered situations, it produces high timber volumes but it is not an important timber tree because the wood is brittle and has few uses. Grand fir is very tolerant of shade and capable of growing slowly under other trees for years and then extending upwards to take advantage of light suddenly available from a break in the leaf canopy overhead. The tree is seldom seen near towns as it cannot tolerate pollution. The very similar European silver fir has been here since the beginning of the 17th century and is among the tallest and largest trees in Britain but it is subject to disease in our wet climate.

✦ 1875

Noble Fir

Abies procera

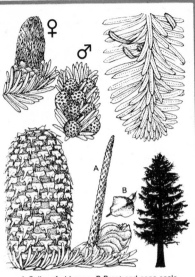

Leaves: flat needles, blue-green on both sides, dense, turning upwards on upper branches. ½ - 1½ in (1-3 cm).

Bark: smooth, silvery grey, few large resin blisters.

Buds: pointed, ovoid, red-brown, small: 2 mm.

Flowers: males deep red, globular, clustered on underside of twig. Females yellow, upright, shaped like a pastry brush.

Cones: very large, green, becoming purplish-brown when ripe with long, down-turned green bracts. Remain upright, central spike left when scales and seeds fall. 6-10 in (15-25 cm).

Shape: conical, with regular whorls of branches.

A-Spike of old cone. B-Bract and cone scale.

This silver fir is one of the many conifers which were introduced from the north-west Pacific coast of America in the middle of the last century, arriving here in 1830. Early introductions were mainly to Scottish estates, particularly in Perthshire, where there are now many large trees. Its formal appearance with straight stem and layers of bluish foliage make noble fir an attractive garden tree but it is seldom seen near large towns. The massive cones, which appear early in life, add to its interest but few seeds are fertile as they are eaten by an insect which was imported with the tree. In its native home it is a mountain tree and it grows well in western Britain, being tolerant of exposure and poor soils. It succeeds at high altitudes but it has a limited use as a timber tree because the wood is not of a very high quality. In Ireland noble fir is used more widely as a forest tree, particularly on dry, upland sites.

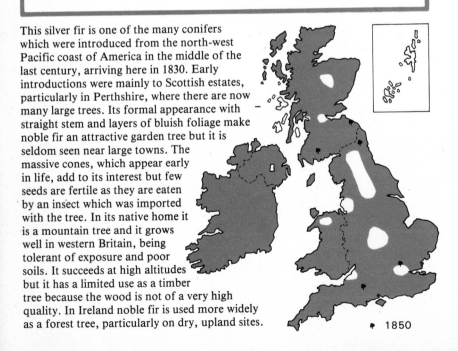

1850

Douglas Fir

Pseudotsuga menziesii

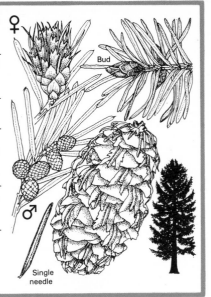

Leaves: flat needles, green, two whitish bands below, parted to show shoot above and below. 1-1½ in (2.5-3 cm).

Bark: smooth, green with resin blisters; becoming brown, corky and thick with deep fissures.

Buds: pointed, shiny-brown like those of beech. ¼ in (6mm).

Flowers: males yellow, scattered on underside of shoots. Females few, deep red, pastry brush-shaped on side of shoots.

Cones: green at first, becoming brown, with long, protruding three-pronged bracts. 3-4in (8-10cm).

Shape: conical. Branchlets with long, hanging foliage. Old trees drop lower branches.

Single needle

Bud

Douglas fir is the most valuable timber tree on the Pacific coast of Canada and the USA. It is fortunate therefore that it has shown excellent growth here since its introduction in 1827; already most of the tallest trees in Britain are Douglas firs. It will grow throughout the country but is at its best in sheltered situations at low altitudes. Sheltered river valleys, where the tree can get its roots down into gravel soil, are the sites where it excels. As the leaves are softer and thinner than other evergreen conifers and are without a hard cuticle, they rot down easily and improve the soil upon which this deep rooting tree grows. Douglas fir has not found its full potential in Britain yet as its high timber quality will make it an ideal tree to follow the first rotation of pioneering larch, pine or spruce, as it will exploit the woodland conditions created by them. It is also found in gardens.

1840

Western Hemlock

Tsuga heterophylla

Leaves: flat needles, dark green with two white bands below. Leaves different sizes giving a scattered appearance. ¼ - ¾ in (6mm - 2cm).

Bark: smooth, purple-brown on young trees; old trees dark brown, deeply fissured.

Buds: minute, grey-brown, hidden by leaves. 2mm.

Flowers: males globular, in dense heads on side shoots. Females purple, at ends of shoots.

Cones: green, hanging down and becoming light brown. Small, with few, rounded scales. ¾ - 1 in (2 - 2.5cm).

Shape: spire-like, with drooping leading shoot and branch tips. Foliage dense.

Leaves of varying length

As this tree grows naturally on the Pacific coast of America with Douglas fir and grand fir, it is not surprising that, like them, it grows well here and seeds freely. It was immediately popular on its introduction in 1851 and became a feature of many large gardens with its graceful branches drooping to the ground, retained even by large trees of which there are now many. Perhaps because it is eclipsed as a timber tree in America by Douglas fir, it was not used in forest plantations here until well into this century. However its timber is useful and it has valuable characteristics which make it suitable for planting under other trees. It will withstand a lot of shade and its drooping leader does not get damaged when pushing up through overhead branches. Thus it mainly occurs as an underplanted crop below larch or enriching poorly stocked hardwood stands.

🌢 1865

Western Red Cedar

Thuja plicata

Leaves: scale-like, broad, in flat sprays. White patches below. Aromatic. ⅛ - ¼ in (3 - 6mm).

Bark: cinnamon red, soft, breaking into long strips which lift off. Base of tree often buttressed.

Flowers: males yellow, minute, on ends of smaller shoots. Females pale green, numerous on older sprays.

Cones: long, green, becoming brown when ripe, with few scales turning back at the tips. ½ in (1 cm).

Shape: conical, upright leading shoot when young; becoming broader with age and with thick branches turned up at the ends. Sometimes layering.

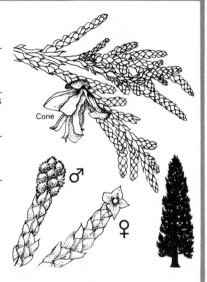

Western red cedar, introduced to Britain in 1853, grows well all over Britain and is at its best in the moist, mild west. Being one of the most shade-tolerant trees that we have, its place in forestry is primarily as an underplanted tree below larch and oak, either to enrich or eventually to follow crops of those species and thereby avoid clearance of the woodland when the older trees are mature. The name—western red cedar—refers to the light, easily worked and very durable wood which cleaves well and is of great importance in Canada as 'cedar shakes and shingles' used for the cladding and roofing of wooden houses. It is imported into Britain for greenhouses and garden sheds and we would do well to grow more of the excellent timber here. It is also a common garden tree, often in one of its golden-leafed forms, and makes an excellent hedge.

1860

Lawson Cypress

Chamaecyparis lawsoniana

Leaves: scale-like, small, in groups of 4 (one pair larger than the other) in flat sprays. Soft, light green, with white streaks below. ¼ in (6mm).

Bark: reddish-brown, smooth in young trees, becoming thick and scaling off in plates.

Flowers: males small, numerous, black at end of branchlets, becoming crimson in spring. Females small, purple-green further back on branchlets.

Cones: green, globular, on short stalks, reddish-brown in autumn. Few hobnail-like scales with small spine in centre. ⅓ in (8mm).

Shape: narrow, leading shoot droops. Dense, hanging foliage. Stem often forked. Many colours and shapes in cultivated varieties.

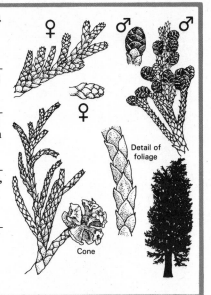

Detail of foliage

Cone

Lawson cypress is named after the nursery firm in Edinburgh that distributed it so widely following its introduction in 1854. It is one of the many fine conifers from north-west America and, while surprisingly restricted there, seems to be more suited to conditions in Britain. It grows well all over the country, except at high elevations and is one of the few evergreen conifers that is not severely affected by dirty town atmospheres. However, it is not a popular forest tree, although the timber is durable, because the stem usually has many forks. Lawson cypress is probably our most common garden tree, certainly our most common garden conifer. There are nearly 100 varieties and cultivars exhibiting a wide range of colours and shapes. These are easily propagated from cuttings and the tree also flowers and seeds well in Britain.

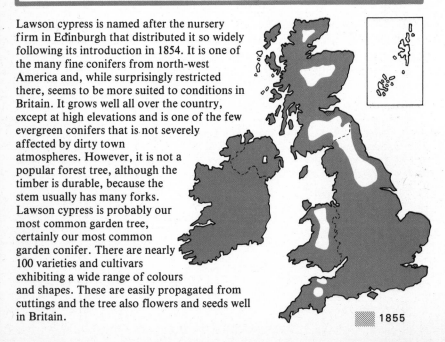

1855

Juniper

Juniperus communis

Leaves: needle-like, sharp, in groups of 3. Blue-green with band of white on upper surface. ½ in (1 cm).

Bark: rich red-brown, curling and flaking off in long thin strips.

Buds: small, with pointed scales. ⅛ in (3 mm).

Flowers: males yellow, globular, on separate trees to females. Females green, small.

Cones: berry-like, green, becoming bluish or purple-black when ripe in second or third year. ¼ in (6 mm).

Shape: variable, usually a bush. Some compact in form, others more spreading. Many cultivated varieties of different shapes and with decorative foliage.

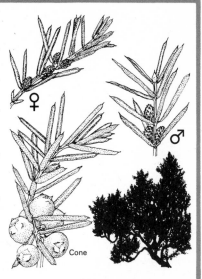

Cone

Juniper is one of our 3 native conifers and was an early pioneer of the barren landscape left as the last of the ice ages receded. It is by no means only confined to Britain and is the most widely distributed coniferous species, occurring in North America, throughout Europe, in north Africa and in Asia. It is more often a large shrub than a tree and in Britain occurs on 2 quite distinct sites: the chalk and limestone of the south-east, and on acid peat soils in pine and birchwoods of the mountainous areas of the north and west. Juniper grows at greater altitudes than any other tree in Britain and reaches the tops of all but the highest mountains, but there it is a procumbent shrub, sometimes distinguished as the sub-species *nana*. Irish juniper 'Hibernica' is the name given to a very narrow form, with upright branches and tight, blue-grey foliage.

2000 BC

Yew

Taxus baccata

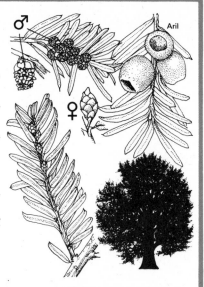

Leaves: flat needles, pointed, dark glossy green above, paler green beneath. Branchlets alternate with brown scales at base. ½ - 1½ in (1 - 3 cm).

Bark: smooth, light-brown, flaking away to leave reddish patches.

Buds: small, with overlapping scales. ⅛ in (3 mm).

Flowers: males small, yellow, globular on underside of shoot, on separate trees to females. Females minute, green, in leaf axils.

Cones: berry-like. The red fleshy 'aril' contains a poisonous seed. ¼ in (6mm).

Shape: single or many stemmed, often with many sprouts near base; broad or spreading crown with hanging branchlets.

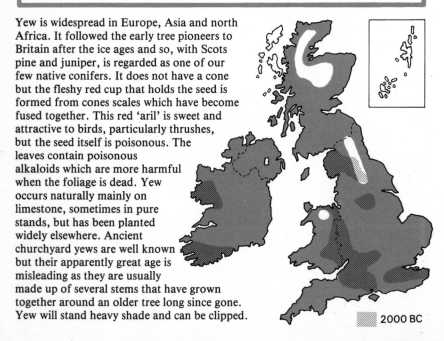

Yew is widespread in Europe, Asia and north Africa. It followed the early tree pioneers to Britain after the ice ages and so, with Scots pine and juniper, is regarded as one of our few native conifers. It does not have a cone but the fleshy red cup that holds the seed is formed from cones scales which have become fused together. This red 'aril' is sweet and attractive to birds, particularly thrushes, but the seed itself is poisonous. The leaves contain poisonous alkaloids which are more harmful when the foliage is dead. Yew occurs naturally mainly on limestone, sometimes in pure stands, but has been planted widely elsewhere. Ancient churchyard yews are well known but their apparently great age is misleading as they are usually made up of several stems that have grown together around an older tree long since gone. Yew will stand heavy shade and can be clipped.

2000 BC

Coast Redwood

Sequoia sempervirens

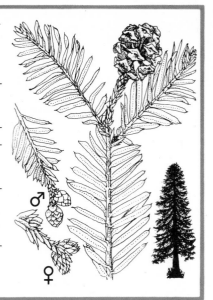

Leaves: flat needles, sharp pointed, bright green above, paler below; in 2 rows exposing green or brown shoots, which are covered with leaves. ¼ - ½ in (6mm - 1cm).

Bark: cinnamon-red to dark brown. Very thick and soft with stringy fibres. Deeply furrowed when old.

Buds: small, green. ⅛ in (3mm).

Flowers: males small, yellow; round at tips of shoots. Females small, green, near ends of shoots.

Cones: small, globular, on stalk-like shoots. Scales thickened on outer edge. Green, becoming red-brown when ripe. ¾ - 1½ in (2-3cm).

Shape: pyramidal, with descending branches. Cut stumps send up coppice shoots.

In their native home on the Coast Ranges of California, these trees grow to great heights and include the tallest trees in the world which are over 350 ft (107 m) and a few reach about 2500 years of age. Brought here in 1843, it thrives in Britain and has been planted widely in parks and large gardens. It likes moisture and some shelter as the leaves are browned by drying winds, so the best growth is in the south-west of this country. Surprisingly coast redwood has hardly been tried as a forest tree although the rate of growth is good and the timber excellent. There is a fast-growing plot at Dartington in Devon and a fine 16-acre stand at Leighton near Welshpool in Wales which includes 33 large trees originally brought from America in 1857 as seedlings in pots. Redwood is one of the few conifers that will sprout coppice shoots from cut stumps and this re-growth will occur even in shade.

1850

Wellingtonia

Sequoiadendron giganteum

Leaves: small, awl-like, curving away from twigs. Dark green. Larger leaves cover shoots. ¼ in (6mm).

Bark: thick, soft, fibrous, light brown. Deeply furrowed.

Buds: minute, covered by leaves.

Flowers: small, round, at ends of shoots; males yellow, females green.

Cones: round, hanging on long stalks. Scales thickened on outer edge with central depression. Green first year, becoming red-brown when ripe in second year. 2-3in (5-8cm).

Shape: tall, spire-like. Descending branches sweep up at tips. Base of trunk buttressed.

Detail of foliage

Wellingtonia, which is closely related to coast redwood, also comes from California but rather further inland. Some very old trees occur there, reaching about 3400 years of age. It was introduced in 1853 and quickly became popular on all large estates. A tradition grew up to plant specimens of Wellingtonia on the boundaries of landed estates so that these were marked out to view from the mansion house, and in many places in the south of England such trees can still be seen. It has also been planted extensively as an avenue tree and as specimens in the lawns of large gardens. Becoming a tall, stately tree of great girth, the spire-like crown is often conspicuous above other trees. Perhaps for this reason, the tops of older trees are frequently dead, often having been struck by lightning. The timber is weak and not durable so plantations have not been established here.

1860

Atlas Cedar

Cedrus atlantica

Leaves: needle-like, dark green (blue in common garden form). Long, single on young shoots, otherwise shorter in rosettes. ¾ - 1 in (2 - 2.5 cm).

Bark: dark grey or black. Cracks into small plates.

Buds: small, brown, round. ⅛ in (3 mm).

Flowers: males yellow, long, ripen in autumn. Females green, erect.

Cones: remain upright. Wasp-nest shape with sunken top. Green first year, then purple to brown when ripe in second year. Scales fall leaving spike. 3 in (8 cm).

Shape: flat top, ascending branches.

Cedar of Lebanon *(Cedrus libani)* differs: branches level; cones larger, top not sunken, 4½ in (11 cm).

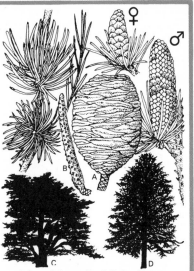

A-Cone. B-Cone spike. C-Cedar of Lebanon. D-Atlas cedar.

Atlas cedar was introduced from the Atlas Mountains of Morocco and Algeria in 1841 and is now popular here in gardens, particularly the blue form 'Glauca'. It is very similar to cedar of Lebanon which was introduced from Turkey in 1638, although most of the largest trees only date back to about 1800. The branching habit is the only real difference, Atlas cedar tending to have ascending branches while cedar of Lebanon usually has level branches. Both cedars like hot, dry conditions so they grow slowly in Britain and are found only as garden and park trees. As would be expected, they are largely confined to the lower and drier parts of the country. In these situations some magnificent trees with great spreading branches occur, particularly on the lawns of large houses where they make magnificent features.

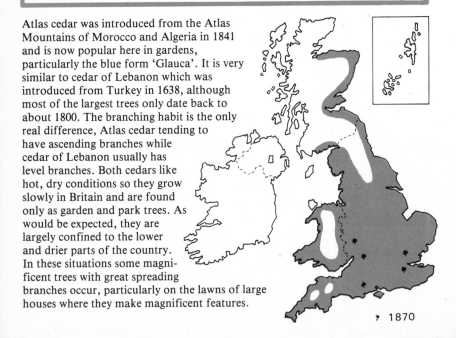

⚲ 1870

Deodar

Cedrus deodara

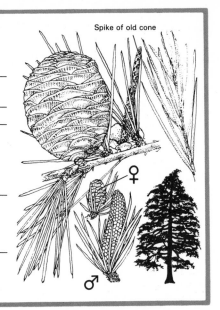

Spike of old cone

Leaves: needle-like, soft, dark green. Long, single on young shoots; shorter and in rosettes on older shoots. 1-1½ in (2.5-3 cm).

Bark: dark grey or black, cracking into plates.

Buds: small, pointed, brown, 1 mm.

Flowers: males yellow, conical, erect, long and curved when ripe in autumn. Females pale green, erect, often on separate trees or separate branches of same tree.

Cones: grey-green in first year. Ripening to dark brown in second. Scales fall leaving central spike. 5½ in (14 cm).

Shape: conical, with drooping leader. Flatter crown when older.

Deodar was introduced to Britain from the Himalayas in 1831 and has become a popular garden tree. Its light green, drooping foliage contrasts well with the darker and stiffer needles of the Atlas cedar and cedar of Lebanon, with which it is often planted. Like them, it is a tree of considerable landscape value so that few large gardens are without good specimens of deodar. In its native home it is a mountain tree and so it is not surprising that deodar is rather more suited to the wetter west of Britain than are the other cedars. In the middle of the last century it was tried as a plantation tree by the Commissioners of Woods and Forests in several Royal Forests with seed obtained from the East India Company. Some remnants of these trials remain in Alice Holt Forest near Farnham and in the New Forest. The growth, however, did not compare with the many North American conifers.

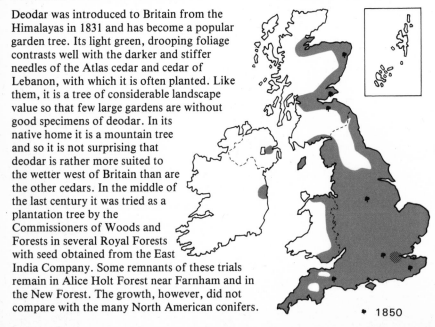

1850

Common Oak

Quercus robur

Leaves: alternate; 4-5 rounded lobes with 'ear' at base. Short-stalked, green above, paler below. Turn russet in autumn. 3-5 in (8-12cm).

Bark: grey, small square plates.

Buds: clustered at shoot tips. Overlapping scales. ¼ in (6mm).

Flowers: males yellow-green catkins. Females green, on long stalks; emerge with young leaves in spring.

Fruit: oval, chestnut brown acorn on long stalks; paired. 1-1½ in (2.5-3cm).

Shape: rounded crown, short trunk. Branches few, arise at same level.

Sessile oak *(Quercus petraea)* differs: crown fan-shaped; branches at different levels; acorns stalkless; leaf-base wedge-shaped, long stalked.

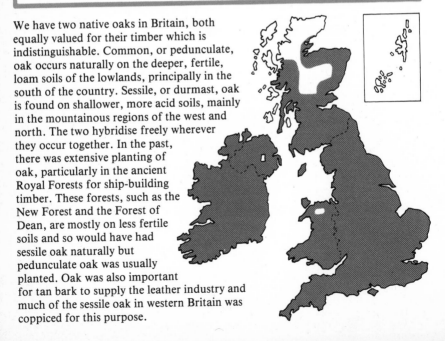

We have two native oaks in Britain, both equally valued for their timber which is indistinguishable. Common, or pedunculate, oak occurs naturally on the deeper, fertile, loam soils of the lowlands, principally in the south of the country. Sessile, or durmast, oak is found on shallower, more acid soils, mainly in the mountainous regions of the west and north. The two hybridise freely wherever they occur together. In the past, there was extensive planting of oak, particularly in the ancient Royal Forests for ship-building timber. These forests, such as the New Forest and the Forest of Dean, are mostly on less fertile soils and so would have had sessile oak naturally but pedunculate oak was usually planted. Oak was also important for tan bark to supply the leather industry and much of the sessile oak in western Britain was coppiced for this purpose.

Holm Oak

Quercus ilex

Leaves: alternate; evergreen, narrow, no teeth. Dark green above, hairy, buff or white below. Young leaves low down on tree holly-like. Stalk woolly. 2-4in (5-10cm).

Bark: ash-grey or black. Cracks into thin scaly plates.

Buds: clustered, very small, pale brown, sometimes with 'whiskers'. ⅛in (3mm).

Flowers: males golden catkins. Females small, green and hairy, on short woolly stalk.

Fruit: oval, green acorn almost half enclosed by cup which has fawn, overlapping, felted scales. ¾in (2cm).

Shape: rounded, broad, dense crown, branching low down. Often more than one trunk.

The actual date of the introduction of holm oak is not accurately known but it was being grown in Britain early in the 16th century. A native of the Mediterranean, where it grows near the sea, it has proved very successful in milder coastal areas of south-west Britain where it has been planted extensively and naturalised itself in many areas. Specimens of this oak are also to be found throughout Britain in parks and gardens, its dense evergreen foliage making it an attractive tree throughout the year. The acorns, which only ripen in good summers, are sweet and mature in the first year, providing food for pheasants and other wildlife, like those of our English oaks. Holm oak withstands clipping and can be used as a hedge. Near the sea it is ideal for providing shelter from salt winds. The young leaves of this oak are often spiny, giving it the alternative name of 'holly oak'.

1600

Turkey Oak

Quercus cerris

Leaves: alternate; dark green, shiny above; hairy below, only on veins as leaf ages. Stipules at base of leaf. Brown in autumn. 3½-5 in (9-12 cm).

Bark: grey with fissures which form small squares.

Buds: ovoid, small, hairy, with long persistent 'whiskers'. ¼ in (6 mm).

Flowers: males yellow-brown catkins, in dense bunches. Females yellow-green, small, in leaf axils.

Fruit: tall, narrow acorn without stalk. Green first summer, ripening brown in second year. Acorn cup 'mossy' with long pointed scales covering half fruit. 1 in (2.5 cm).

Shape: upright branches form a wide crown.

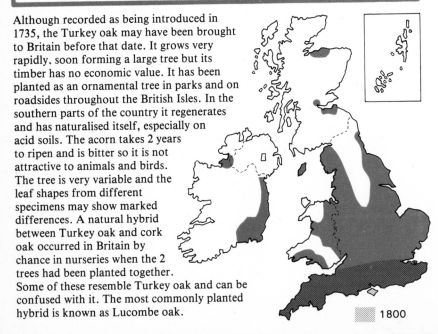

Although recorded as being introduced in 1735, the Turkey oak may have been brought to Britain before that date. It grows very rapidly, soon forming a large tree but its timber has no economic value. It has been planted as an ornamental tree in parks and on roadsides throughout the British Isles. In the southern parts of the country it regenerates and has naturalised itself, especially on acid soils. The acorn takes 2 years to ripen and is bitter so it is not attractive to animals and birds. The tree is very variable and the leaf shapes from different specimens may show marked differences. A natural hybrid between Turkey oak and cork oak occurred in Britain by chance in nurseries when the 2 trees had been planted together. Some of these resemble Turkey oak and can be confused with it. The most commonly planted hybrid is known as Lucombe oak.

1800

Red Oak

Quercus borealis

Leaves: alternate; lobes tipped with teeth ending in fine bristles, deep indentations between. Matt-green above and below. Autumn colour red-orange. 4-8in (10-20cm).

Bark: shiny grey when young; becoming dark and broken by fissures into broad flat ridges with age.

Buds: dark brown, pointed, ovoid. ¼ in (6mm).

Flowers: males slender, yellow-green catkins. Females small, red, in leaf axils.

Fruit: squat, round acorn. Green first year, ripening dark red-brown second year. Cup wide and flat, scales edged purple. 1in (2.5cm).

Shape: branches form open, domed crown.

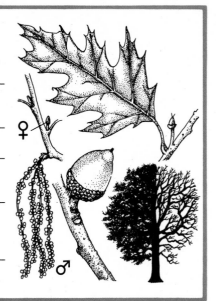

Red oak was introduced in 1724 and comes from the eastern regions of North America. In America it is a light-demanding tree occurring on well-drained soils with birch, aspen and pine. In Britain it is the most successful of the many North American oaks, several of which are planted for their brilliant autumn colour. It is common in parks and has been planted for amenity along the edges of conifer plantations. It is not a timber tree like our own oaks as it does not get to the same size, nor is the wood as durable. In some areas in Britain, red oak has seeded itself naturally but the acorns do not ripen regularly as they do on the Continent where the tree has become naturalised. Like most of the oaks that take 2 years to ripen their seed, the acorns of red oak are bitter and are not as attractive to wildlife as are those of our own oaks.

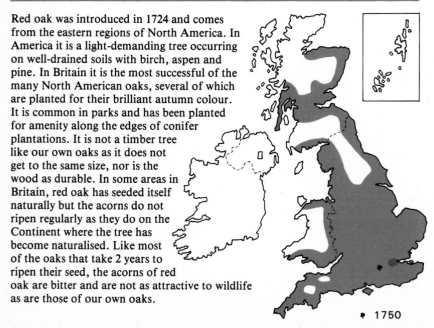

1750

Ash

Fraxinus excelsior

Leaves: opposite; 9-13 leaflets, laterals small stalked, terminal leaflet longer stalked. Teeth point forward. Green above, paler below, white hairs on main vein. Comes into leaf late. 10 in (25 cm).

Bark: greenish-grey when young. Old trees grey, with thick ridges.

Buds: large, black, shaped like a bishop's mitre. 2-4 in (5-10 cm).

Flowers: males and females purple, emerging before the leaves, on same tree or often on separate trees.

Fruit: single seeds on twisted wing, in dense bunches of 'keys'. Green at first, ripening to pale brown. 1½ in (3 cm).

Shape: tall, open tree, long trunk with ascending branches.

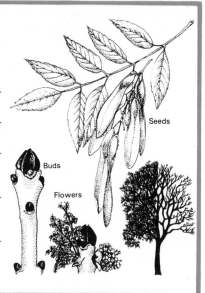

Seeds

Buds

Flowers

Although ash occurs throughout the British Isles, it grows best on rich deep soils and forms pure woodlands on limestone. After birch and willow, it was one of the earliest hardwoods to establish itself following the retreat of the ice as it produces abundant seed which germinates freely. The seedlings require shade and protection from grazing animals to establish themselves but the mature tree requires plenty of light. The sparse foliage allows sunlight to reach the ground so that a rich and varied ground cover is found in ashwoods, including some rare orchids. As a result, such woods are rich in insect life. Ash is not a long-lived tree but it coppices freely and soon appears in cut-over woodland from remaining stumps. Although ash regenerates abundantly on dry, limestone sites, when grown commercially for its timber the tree has to be planted on very fertile soils.

2000 BC

Alder

Alnus glutinosa

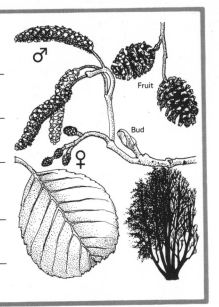

Leaves: alternate; wavy edged, few small teeth. Tip rounded, sometimes notched. Dark green above, paler below, hairy on veins. 4in (10cm).

Bark: dark brown, rough, cracking into small plates. When cut, exposed wood turns orange.

Buds: club-shaped, stalked, purple. One large scale hides the rest. 2½ in (6cm).

Flowers: males long purple catkins, present all winter, ripen before leaves emerge. Females small, brown, round, on same tree.

Fruit: round, cone-like, green at first, turning woody brown. Stay on tree all winter. 3-6in (8-15cm).

Shape: conical; open foliage with regular branches. Often bushy.

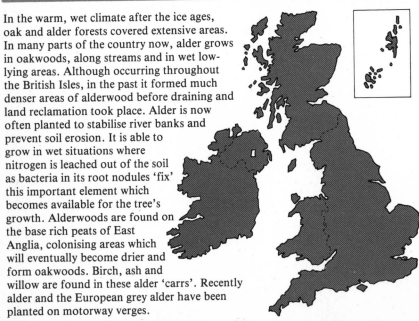

In the warm, wet climate after the ice ages, oak and alder forests covered extensive areas. In many parts of the country now, alder grows in oakwoods, along streams and in wet low-lying areas. Although occurring throughout the British Isles, in the past it formed much denser areas of alderwood before draining and land reclamation took place. Alder is now often planted to stabilise river banks and prevent soil erosion. It is able to grow in wet situations where nitrogen is leached out of the soil as bacteria in its root nodules 'fix' this important element which becomes available for the tree's growth. Alderwoods are found on the base rich peats of East Anglia, colonising areas which will eventually become drier and form oakwoods. Birch, ash and willow are found in these alder 'carrs'. Recently alder and the European grey alder have been planted on motorway verges.

Rowan

Sorbus aucuparia

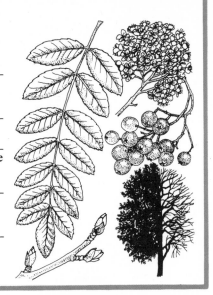

Leaves: alternate; 9-15 stalkless leaflets with sharp, forward pointing teeth. Dark green above, paler below; turn orange-brown in autumn. 8 in (20 cm).

Bark: smooth, shiny, grey with pale breathing pores. Becomes rougher with age.

Buds: ovoid, dark brown, hairy. ½ in (1 cm).

Flowers: male and female parts in same flower. Creamy-white petals in dense woolly heads in May.

Fruit: berries in heads; green, turning yellow, orange or red when ripe. Attractive to birds. ¾ in (2 cm).

Shape: small, slender tree with few ascending branches, forming narrow open crown.

Rowan is commonly found on the more acid soils of the north and west of Britain where the climate is wet. In other parts of the country it has probably been introduced and, together with rowans from the Far East, is planted as a garden and roadside tree. In such situations it thrives on a wide variety of soils and will grow on chalk. Rowan is a very hardy tree and resistant to the wind, surviving higher up mountainsides than any other deciduous tree. In the north of England and in Scotland it is associated with birch and pine, colonising open ground and requiring plenty of light. Like many pioneer species, it grows quickly but is not long-lived. It seeds freely and is spread by birds who feed on the palatable berries. In areas where rowan and whitebeam grow together, hybrids occur with partly divided leaves, and several other forms have been produced artificially for street planting.

2000 BC

Whitebeam

Sorbus aria

Leaves: alternate; oval, green above, white below, very hairy. Margin double toothed; few teeth towards leaf base. 9-12 pairs of parallel veins. Autumn brown or gold. 2-4in (5-10cm).

Bark: smooth, light grey, pale breathing pores, rougher with age.

Buds: ovoid, brown with white hairy tip. ¾in (2cm).

Flowers: male and female parts in same flower. Creamy-white petals, many flowers in dense heads in May; sweet scented.

Fruit: berries in heads; green, becoming scarlet when ripe. Attractive to birds. ½in (1cm).

Shape: upswept branches form compact, dense crown.

A-White underside of leaf.

The natural range of the whitebeam is mainly on the chalks and limestones of southern Britain where it is locally common. As a planted tree, however, its range has been considerably extended; it has been used as a street and roadside tree in many areas. It is especially useful in such situations as it is adapted for living on dry soils and the hairy thick leaves reduce water loss. Trees planted in streets often suffer from lack of water and from reflected sunlight from surrounding surfaces and these conditions are very similar to those prevailing in the whitebeam's natural surroundings. It is a variable tree in the wild and a number of related forms with restricted ranges are to be found. Cultivars have also been developed artificially for ornamental planting, for their attractive leaves and fruit. The berries are eaten by birds and the seeds, when dropped, germinate.

2000 BC

Aspen

Populus tremula

Leaves: alternate; round, thin; margin wavy. Glossy green above, paler below; yellow in autumn. Long flattened leaf stalks cause leaves to flutter. 1½ - 2½ in (3-6cm).

Bark: greenish white with diamond-shaped markings. Furrowed at base in old trees.

Buds: brown, sticky. ¼ in (6mm).

Flowers: male catkins brown, ripening yellow. Female catkins green or purple. On separate trees emerging before the leaves.

Fruit: catkins of fluffy seeds on female trees only; fall late May. Seeds spread by wind.

Shape: conical, with light, open branches. Suckers freely so trees occur in groups.

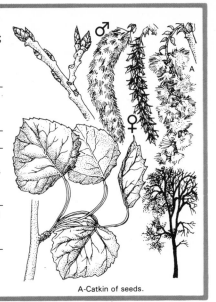

A-Catkin of seeds.

This tree is not well known but it occurs throughout the British Isles. It is a pioneer on a wide range of sites from the Scottish Highlands to the gravel soils of the New Forest in Hampshire. Nowhere is it particularly abundant but it is more common in the north and west. Although it is a poplar, it does not need the moist conditions usually associated with those trees. It often occurs in clumps in woodlands or on the edges of them as it regenerates as much by suckers arising from the spreading roots as from seed. Aspen can be regarded as a truly native tree as it was here before the ice ages and quickly returned after them. It is a small tree with soft wood and can be cut down easily so that the number of trees present now is probably a lot less than in the past. It is only totally absent from towns and industrial areas.

2000 BC

Black Poplar

Populus nigra

Leaves: alternate; triangular, pointed. Longer than broad; small regular teeth. glossy green above, paler below, margin pale. Stalk flat. 2½ in (6 cm).

Bark: grey-brown; network of ridges.

Buds: long, pointed. ½ in (1 cm).

Flowers: male catkins crimson, female catkins green. On separate trees. Open March, before leaves.

Fruit: catkins of fluffy white seeds, falling in June.

Shape: few heavy branches arch downwards forming a wide crown. Trunk often has burrs at base.

Lombardy poplar (*P. nigra* 'italica') differs: narrow, upright shape; fluted trunk; leaf broader than long. Only male trees occur in Britain.

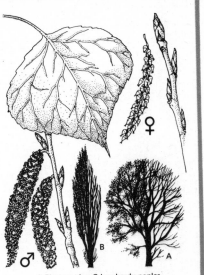

A-Black poplar. B-Lombardy poplar.

Black poplar is probably a native tree, at least in Lancashire and Cheshire and possibly in east and central England as well. It has been planted in the north-west of England to screen buildings and there it is often called 'Manchester poplar'. It does not get as large as the many hybrid poplars that have arisen from the crossing of the European black poplar with the North American black poplar and which have much straighter stems. They all grow well on low-lying, fertile ground, particularly in the Fens where they are sometimes planted along field boundaries. They need moisture but the site must be flushed with moving water which is well aerated, not stagnant. The well-known Lombardy poplar is a cultivar of black poplar that first arose in the middle of the 18th century in Lombardy in northern Italy. It has been planted widely here, often in straight rows to hide buildings.

1765

Grey Poplar

Populus canescens

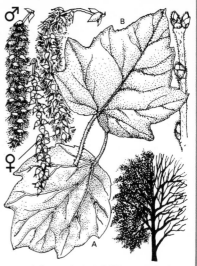

Leaves: alternate; round, thick. Grey-green above; grey, hairy below. Toothed. Flat stalk. 2½-3½ in (6-9 cm).

Bark: lower trunk black, heavily ridged; upper bark greenish white, pitted with black diamonds.

Buds: brown, ovoid. ½ in (1 cm).

Flowers: male catkins grey or purple. Female green, seldom seen, on separate trees in March.

Fruit: catkins of fluffy white seeds falling in May.

Shape: tall tree with open crown and large branches.

White poplar *(Populus alba)* differs: leaf lobed, white hairs below; bud very hairy; smaller tree, light branches; suckers freely.

A-Grey poplar leaf. B-White poplar leaf.

White poplar has been grown in Britain for a long time and may have been introduced by the Romans. By the 17th century it was being planted extensively in parks and gardens here. Now it is often found growing on sandy coasts where it reproduces itself by suckers, providing useful shelter against salt winds. Grey poplar is very similar and thought to be a hybrid between white poplar and aspen, as the variable leaf shape can resemble either of these trees. Its range is more extensive than white poplar and is found further to the north and west. It occurs in damp oakwoods and river valleys. Like white poplar, it is also often plant-ed by the sea. Although grey poplar is sometimes thought to be a native tree, it is common on the Continent and it seems more likely that it first arose there since aspen and white poplar occur frequently together in Europe.

Western Balsam Poplar

Populus trichocarpa

Leaves: alternate; thick, large, triangular, small regular teeth. Green above, metallic-white below, turning yellow in autumn. 4-10in (10-25 cm).

Bark: green, smooth, becoming grey, breaking into shallow cracks when older.

Buds: large, pointed, brown, sticky, with sweet smell. 1½ in (3 cm).

Flowers: male catkins dull crimson, female catkins green, on separate trees, ripen in April before leaves.

Fruit: catkins on female trees only; break up into white, fluffy seeds in May.

Shape: numerous branches produce conical shape. On older trees, canker produces black swellings on twigs and branches with much dead wood.

Catkin of seeds

Western balsam poplar, introduced in 1892, is the cottonwood of north-west America, so named because of its fluffy white seeds which fall as long catkins in late spring. Like the north-west American conifers with which it occurs naturally, it grows well in western Britain, particularly at low altitudes. Balsam poplar tolerates more acid and less fertile soils than other poplars and so has a use as a plantation tree on low-lying sites in the north and west. Unfortunately balsam poplar is very susceptible to a bacterial canker of the stem and branches which restricts growth and disfigures the tree. However poplars hybridise easily so that it has been possible to cross this tree with more resistant poplars, both eastern balsam (also from America) and black poplars, to produce canker-free strains with the tolerance of western balsam poplar.

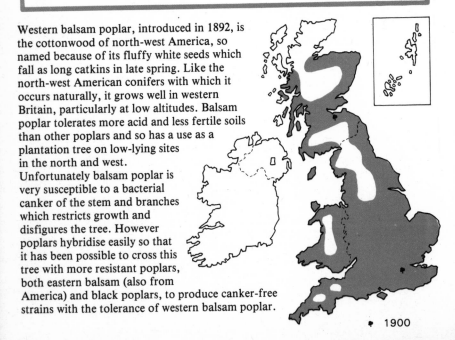

1900

Goat Willow

Salix caprea

Leaves: alternate; oval, short pointed; round base; margin wavy. Dark green above, woolly with dense grey hairs below. Leaf stalk hairy, red. 2½-4in (6-10cm).

Bark: smooth, grey, with shallow fissures near base.

Buds: ovoid, pointed, bright red. Hairy when young, becoming shiny. ¼ in (6mm).

Flowers: males oval, covered with silky hairs, then yellow stamens when ripe, before leaves. Females similar, larger than males with green styles; insect pollinated.

Fruit: conical, green, ripening to fluffy seeds which are shed in May.

Shape: small, low, bushy tree with rounded crown.

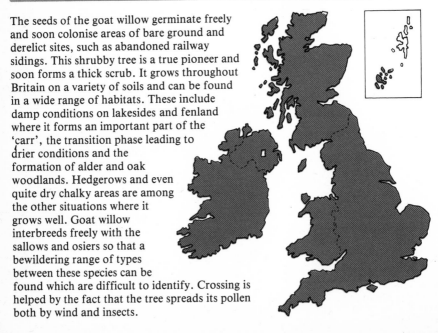

The seeds of the goat willow germinate freely and soon colonise areas of bare ground and derelict sites, such as abandoned railway sidings. This shrubby tree is a true pioneer and soon forms a thick scrub. It grows throughout Britain on a variety of soils and can be found in a wide range of habitats. These include damp conditions on lakesides and fenland where it forms an important part of the 'carr', the transition phase leading to drier conditions and the formation of alder and oak woodlands. Hedgerows and even quite dry chalky areas are among the other situations where it grows well. Goat willow interbreeds freely with the sallows and osiers so that a bewildering range of types between these species can be found which are difficult to identify. Crossing is helped by the fact that the tree spreads its pollen both by wind and insects.

White Willow

Salix alba

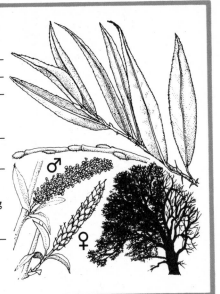

Leaves: alternate; long, pointed; small regular teeth. Grey-green above, hairy, dense white hairs below. 3 in (8 cm).	

Bark: dark grey, network of ridges.

Buds: fawn, hairy. 2 mm.

Flowers: male catkins yellow, female catkins green, on separate trees, ripen when leaves emerge in April.

Fruit: catkin of fluffy white seeds, ripen June.

Shape: ascending branches from narrow irregular white-leafed crown. Forms of white willow include weeping willows and cricket-bat willow. White and crack willows often pollarded.

Crack willow *(Salix fragilis)* differs: broad open crown; twigs break easily; leaves not hairy below.

The distribution of white willow and the similar crack willow overlap. Both occur naturally by rivers, on marshland and in damp woods throughout the British Isles, with the exception of north Scotland. They have been planted extensively to stabilise river banks and prevent erosion and they are often pollarded in these situations. Like the goat willow, these willows invade drying fenland to form 'carr', together with alder, birch and ash. Crosses between these two willows occur and are fairly common, giving rise to a number of intermediate forms. White willow is a variable tree itself. One of its better known forms is the cricket-bat willow, still grown in East Anglia for this purpose under very specialised conditions. Other forms of white willow and its hybrids have been selected for their ornamental value. The commonest is the attractive yellow-twigged weeping willow.

2000 BC

Silver Birch

Betula pendula

Leaves: alternate; triangular, thin, double-toothed, some teeth much larger than others. 1-2½ in (2.5-6cm).

Bark: shiny brown when young, becoming black, rough at base. Upper bark white with black diamonds.

Buds: small, green or brown, pointed. ¼ in (6mm).

Flowers: male catkins brown, females smaller, green. Present all winter, ripen April before leaves.

Fruit: green catkins, ripening brown, breaking into small, winged seeds.

Shape: young trees conical; long pendulous branches when old.

Downy birch *(Betula pubescens)* differs: bark has no diamonds; leaf has regular teeth; branches not so pendulous; twigs hairy.

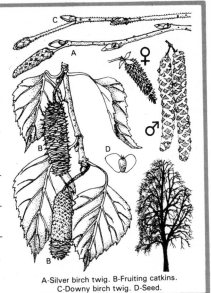

A-Silver birch twig. B-Fruiting catkins. C-Downy birch twig. D-Seed.

Birch was one of the first deciduous trees to invade Britain after the ice ages. Its small, light seeds enable it to spread rapidly and colonise disturbed or bare ground. It grows fast and is short-lived, helping to improve conditions for and protect the seedlings of the more long-lived trees that follow. Birch occurs as 2 main species in Britain: silver birch which grows on light soils in dry areas, and downy birch which grows in wetter and cooler conditions. The latter is, therefore, more commonly found in the north and west and is a variable species with a wide range of leaf forms, the leaves of the northern forms generally being smaller. Birch does not cast a heavy shade so that it allows ground vegetation to flourish, thus providing an important habitat for many birds, animals and plants. In young forestry plantations, birch is often left as browse for deer.

Beech

Fagus sylvatica

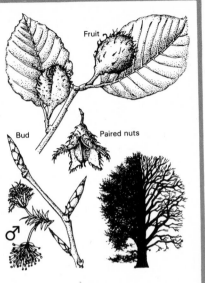

Fruit

Bud

Paired nuts

♂

Leaves: alternate; oval, dark shiny green above, paler below. 6-7 parallel veins. Leaf margin wavy. Orange or brown in autumn. 4in (10cm).

Bark: smooth, grey.

Buds: light brown, slender, long pointed. ¾ in (2cm).

Flowers: males are bunches of yellow stamens. Females round, green, on same tree, emerging at the same time as the leaves.

Fruit: prickly, 4-valved husk contains 2 edible triangular nutlets. 1in (2.5cm).

Shape: conical, tall, slender trunk; without branches when grown close together; heavy branches and spreading in open situations.

If beech is native, it is the most recent tree to get to Britain on its own. It arrived during the Bronze Age several thousand years after man; it has an edible nut so may well have been introduced as feed for domestic animals. It is now the dominant tree on the chalk and limestone soil of the south-east and, whether introduced or native there, has spread and been planted throughout Britain on to all but the highest mountains. After good summers when the seed ripens well, beech seedlings occur where the forest floor is clear of competing vegetation. Traditionally beechwoods have been managed to make use of this natural regeneration by felling mature trees in small groups where it occurs. Beech casts a dense shade and allows little light to filter through the leafy canopy so that there is only sparse ground vegetation. This in turn restricts the wildlife and birds in particular.

400 BC

Hornbeam

Carpinus betulus

Leaves: alternate; oval, double
toothed. 15 pairs of parallel veins.
Dark green, shiny above, paler below.
Muddy brown in autumn.
3-4in (8-10cm).

Bark: smooth, silver grey.

Buds: slender, brown, pointed, with
many scales lying close to zig-zag twigs.
¼ in (6mm).

Flowers: male catkins yellow-green.
Female catkins leafy green. Open same
time as young leaves.

Fruit: bunch of brown nutlets, each
enclosed in 3-pronged wing.
½ in (1cm).

Shape: young trees bushy, broad, often
with fluted trunk when old. Many old
trees have been pollarded or coppiced.

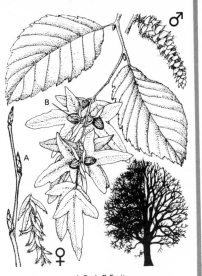

A-Bud. B-Fruit.

Like beech, hornbeam arrived in Britain in the
Bronze Age. If it is a native tree, it is certainly
only so in south-east England and possibly
small areas in the south-west. It has been
planted throughout England and Wales and
into eastern Scotland. There are occasional
pure stands but more often it occurs in
beechwoods where, as a shade-bearer, it forms
an understorey and never gets large. Old
trees have usually been pollarded
in the past to supply browse for
stock that could be grown out of
reach and then the leaves fed to
the stock by lopping off the
pollard shoots. Hornbeam was
also an important source of
firewood for London and some
old pollards in the Home
Counties, particularly in Epping
Forest, are remnants of this use. Nowadays
it is an ornamental tree, particularly as the cultivar
'Fastigiata' and has long been used as a hedge.

400 BC

Crab Apple

Malus sylvestris

Leaves: alternate; oval, toothed. Dark green above, woolly with white hairs below when young. Not persisting when old as in cultivated apples. 1 - 1½ in (2.5 - 3 cm).

Bark: dark, grey-brown, cracking to form small plates.

Buds: purple-brown, hairy, on thorny twigs. ¼ in (6 mm).

Flowers: males and females in same flower with 5 white petals, often pinkish; open May with leaves.

Fruit: small apple, green, then red when ripe. Bitter in truly wild trees. Used for preserves. 1 in (2.5 cm).

Shape: low, broad tree or shrub with numerous, dense branches. Often leaning.

A-Long shoot. B-Short shoot.

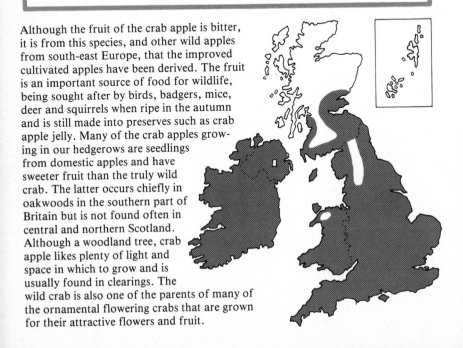

Although the fruit of the crab apple is bitter, it is from this species, and other wild apples from south-east Europe, that the improved cultivated apples have been derived. The fruit is an important source of food for wildlife, being sought after by birds, badgers, mice, deer and squirrels when ripe in the autumn and is still made into preserves such as crab apple jelly. Many of the crab apples growing in our hedgerows are seedlings from domestic apples and have sweeter fruit than the truly wild crab. The latter occurs chiefly in oakwoods in the southern part of Britain but is not found often in central and northern Scotland. Although a woodland tree, crab apple likes plenty of light and space in which to grow and is usually found in clearings. The wild crab is also one of the parents of many of the ornamental flowering crabs that are grown for their attractive flowers and fruit.

London Plane

Platanus x *hispanica*

Leaves: alternate; 5 lobes with pointed tips and few curved teeth. Bright green above, paler below. 5½ in (14cm).

Bark: smooth, grey, flaking to leave large yellow patches.

Buds: ovoid, red-brown, tip curved. ¼ in (6mm).

Flowers: male catkins in 2-3 round heads containing many flowers; yellow. Females similar, reddish. Open with leaves, May.

Fruit: round, spiky, 'bobble'-like fruits, long stalks. Green, ripening brown, remain all winter. 1 in (2.5cm).

Shape: large spreading branches form broad crown. Street trees often lopped into ugly shapes.

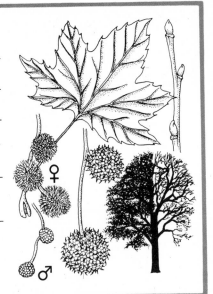

The London plane is considered to be a hybrid between two species brought together by man from widely separated regions: the oriental plane from south-east Europe and the American plane from the United States, which were introduced as ornamental trees. There is evidence to suggest that both were grown by the famous gardeners, the Tradescants, in their London nurseries. The first recorded London plane was described in the Oxford Botanic Gardens about 1670 and, as the Tradescants sent plants to stock those gardens, that specimen may have come from them. The London plane is a vigorous hybrid and has proved itself an excellent tree to grow in polluted atmospheres, especially in London. Its habit of shedding bark in large patches enables it to get rid of soot and other harmful substances which accumulate on the stem and branches.

1700

Sycamore

Acer pseudoplatanus

Leaves: opposite; 5 lobes, margin with large irregular teeth. Dark green above, paler below. 5½ in (14 cm).

Bark: smooth, grey-green, becoming scaly when old.

Buds: large, ovoid, green scales with black margin. ½ in (1 cm).

Flowers: male and female parts in same flower, in long hanging bunches. 5 small greenish-yellow petals. Open with leaves, May.

Fruit: paired seeds, each enclosed in a wing, hang in bunches. Green, ripening brown, small angle between wings. 1½ in (3 cm).

Shape: large tree; broad, rounded, dense, spreading crown, especially in open situations.

It is not known how long this surprisingly unpopular tree has been in Britain and whether it is a native. It is, however, well suited to conditions here and grows excellently all over the country, including high and exposed places. On some Scottish islands sycamore has been planted to provide shelter around farmhouses where almost no other trees will grow. Sycamore regenerates more freely than any other tree in Britain and dense crops of seedlings occur wherever the soil is rich and the site bare. It is often the first tree to re-colonise derelict sites and it coppices from cut stumps. Both the trees arising from seedlings, known as 'maidens', and those from coppice shoots, quickly form pure woodland with few other species present. It is sometimes claimed that sycamore is devoid of wildlife but all woodlands, particularly deciduous woodlands, provide excellent habitats.

Norway Maple

Acer platanoides

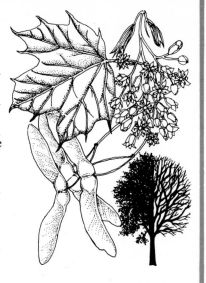

Leaves: opposite; 5-7 lobes. Thin, wavy, edged with few, long pointed teeth. Shiny, bright green above and below. Yellow in autumn. 2-6in (5-15cm).

Bark: smooth, light brown with shallow fissures.

Buds: large, ovoid; scales green with brown margins. ¼ in (6mm).

Flowers: male and female parts in same flower. 5 yellow-green petals. Small groups of flowers in upright heads, opening before leaves.

Fruit: single seed enclosed in wing, in pairs, hanging in bunches. Angle between wings wider than sycamore. Green, ripening brown. 2in (5cm).

Shape: broad, spreading crown, not as dense as sycamore.

Although common in the more mountainous areas throughout Europe, the Norway maple was not recorded in Britain until its introduction from the Caucasus in 1683. It is a hardy tree growing well here and has naturalised itself in some areas. Its use in this country is as an ornamental tree only, being planted both for its yellow flowers, appearing early in the year before the leaves emerge, and for the colour of its autumn leaves. Various cultivars of the tree can be found in gardens which differ in their leaf colours, from variegated green and white forms to purple- or red-leafed trees. Norway maple can be found in gardens, parks and on roadsides throughout Britain, though it is not so common in the north. Like other maples, the sap is rich in sugar, especially in the spring and, in the past, trees were tapped for their sugar in Europe.

1690

Field Maple

Acer campestre

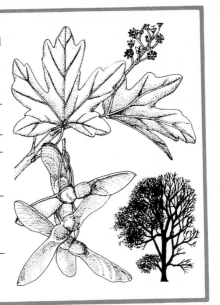

Leaves: opposite; 5-7 lobes. Margin entire or few blunt, rounded teeth. Dull green above, paler and hairy below. Stalks long, red. Emerging leaves red. Gold, red or brown in autumn. 2¾ in (7cm).

Bark: smooth, grey, becoming rough in older trees.

Buds: brown, tip hairy. ¼ in (6mm).

Flowers: males and females in same flower. Few pale green flowers in upright heads, opening with leaves.

Fruit: paired seeds, each enclosed in a wing, hanging in bunches. Wings in straight line. Yellow-green with red streaks. 1 in (2.5cm).

Shape: small tree with rounded crown. Often has burrs on the trunk.

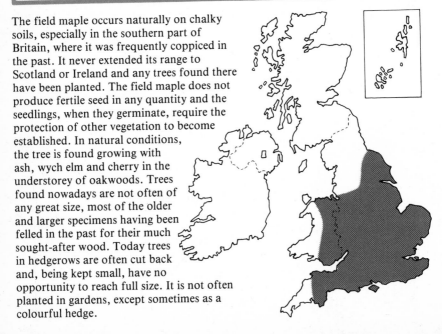

The field maple occurs naturally on chalky soils, especially in the southern part of Britain, where it was frequently coppiced in the past. It never extended its range to Scotland or Ireland and any trees found there have been planted. The field maple does not produce fertile seed in any quantity and the seedlings, when they germinate, require the protection of other vegetation to become established. In natural conditions, the tree is found growing with ash, wych elm and cherry in the understorey of oakwoods. Trees found nowadays are not often of any great size, most of the older and larger specimens having been felled in the past for their much sought-after wood. Today trees in hedgerows are often cut back and, being kept small, have no opportunity to reach full size. It is not often planted in gardens, except sometimes as a colourful hedge.

Common Lime

Tilia x *europaea*

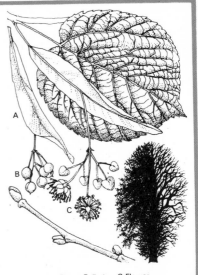

Leaves: alternate; heart-shaped, thin. Toothed. Dull green above, paler below; tufts of hairs in vein axils. Stalk green, not hairy. Yellow in autumn. 2½ - 4 in (6 - 10 cm).

Bark: smooth, grey, becoming ridged. Many sprouts and burrs.

Buds: ovoid, red-brown. Scales, one large, one small. ½ in (1 cm).

Flowers: male and female in same flower. 4 - 10 yellow flowers with green bracts hang in bunches. Scented.

Fruit: ovoid, faintly ribbed, hairy. Often infertile, clustered. ¼ in (6 mm).

Shape: arching branches form broad, spreading crown. Often lopped in towns.

A-Bract. B-Fruit   C-Flower.

The origin of common lime is unknown but it is generally accepted as a hybrid between large-leafed lime and small-leafed lime, both of which occur naturally in Britain. When and how the cross occurred is unknown, or whether it was in Britain or on the Continent. Interest in planting limes increased after the gardens laid out at Versailles by Louis XIV showed what could be achieved. In the 18th century lime was in great demand for planting as an avenue tree in parks throughout Britain and many were imported from nurseries in Flanders. Like English elm, these were propagated vegetatively by layering. This resulted in trees of even growth and similar shape which were ideal for avenue planting. The tree is still popular for such planting and for lining streets; however it is often lopped and sometimes mutilated to keep it within bounds.

English Elm

Ulmus procera

Leaves: alternate; oval; base lopsided; short pointed, double teeth. Thick, rough, hairy. Dark green above, paler below. Yellow in autumn. 4 in (10 cm).

Bark: dark grey-brown, cracking into network of ridges.

Bud: ovoid, brown. 2 mm.

Flowers: males and females in same flower; coloured red by bunches of stamens; open March before leaves.

Fruit: round wing with notched tip contains single seed above centre. Green, ripens brown. Hang in dense bunches. Usually sterile. ¾ in (2 cm).

Shape: tall, domed tree with few large branches. Foliage dense, forming rounded layers. Numerous suckers at base of trunk.

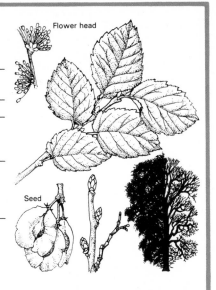

Flower head

Seed

Although regarded as typical of the landscape of lowland England, the origin of this magnificent tree is a matter for speculation. It seems that English elm was selected for its attractive shape, and many trees from Flanders were imported to be planted in the hedgerows of Britain during the enclosures. English elm does not often set fertile seed, but is easily propagated vegetatively in nurseries, while trees in hedgerows have spread by root suckers. This means that it only occurs in the areas where it was originally planted in lowland Britain. Because the elm population is derived from comparatively few parent trees and lacks the variability of a natural population, a virulent strain of elm disease introduced in 1967 has spread rapidly, devastating English elms over much of southern Britain. However, there is no reason to believe that all the elms will be destroyed.

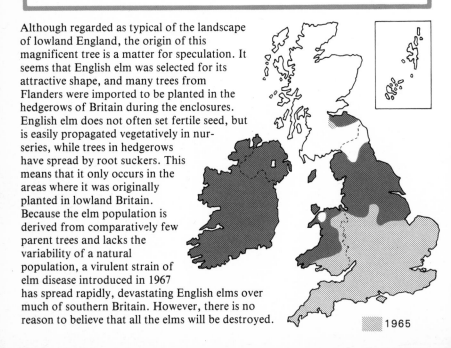

1965

Wych Elm

Ulmus glabra

Leaves: alternate; oval, larger than other elms. Base unequal, longer side covers short stalk. Double teeth. Dark green, rough above, paler below, hairy on veins. 4-7in (10-18cm).

Bark: smooth, grey-brown when young, cracking into vertical fissures.

Buds: ovoid, large, red-brown, hairy. ¼ in (6mm).

Flowers: both sexes in same flower. Coloured purplish-red by stamens in March, open before leaves.

Fruit: single central seed contained in round wing with notched tip. Hang in bunches, brown. ¾ in (2cm).

Shape: broad, rounded crown. Burrs and sprouts occur on the short trunk. Does not sucker.

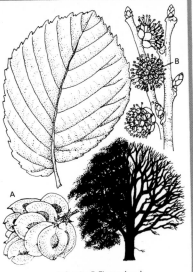

A-Seeds. B-Flower head.

Pollen grains in the peats from the boreal period after the ice receded belonged to the wych elm. It formed part of the tree cover, together with oak and ash, at that period when conditions began to get warmer after the Ice Age. It still grows in association with these trees today, occurring throughout the British Isles, especially in northern oakwoods and in ashwoods on limestone. It is the only native elm found in Ireland, having colonised that country before its separation from the rest of Britain. Unlike other elms, it does not reproduce by suckering but sets abundant fertile seed, thus ensuring its wide distribution. The fact that it does not sucker means that the population is more variable than English elm. As it tolerates pollution, it is often planted in town parks. Its resistance to salt winds and exposure make it a useful tree for planting in exposed situations.

Horse Chestnut

Aesculus hippocastanum

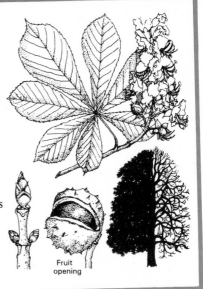

Leaves: opposite; thick, 5-7 stalkless leaflets, narrow at base, broadening to tip. Toothed. Dark green above, paler below. Leaf scar on twig like horseshoe. 3-8 in (8-20 cm).

Bark: red-brown, small scaly plates.

Buds: large, red-brown, pointed, sticky. ¼-1½ in (6 mm-3 cm).

Flowers: males and females in same flower; also male flowers only. Many white flowers borne in long spikes ('candles') in May, open after leaves emerge in April.

Fruit: round, prickly green case contains 2-3 round, mahogany-coloured fruits ('conkers'). 2½ in (6 cm).

Shape: few heavy branches up-turned at ends. Often layer round old trees. Rounded, broad crown.

Fruit opening

Horse chestnut, with its 'candles' of flowers in the spring and its 'conkers' in the autumn, is such a familiar tree to everyone that it is difficult to remember that, in fact, it has only been part of the British landscape for less than 400 years. It was introduced from the Balkans in 1616 as an ornamental tree for use in formal avenues. It is planted now throughout Britain, both for its striking flowers which provide a source of nectar for insects and bees in spring and for its value as a shade tree on roadsides and avenues. It has naturalised itself in most parts of the country as it produces fertile seed freely. In places where damage to trees from 'conker' gatherers is a problem, an infertile form, with double white flowers but producing no fruit, can be planted. A cross between horse chestnut and the red buckeye, from North America, resulted in the hybrid red horse chestnut.

🌳 1700

Sweet Chestnut

Castanea sativa

Leaves: alternate; long with sharp spiny teeth. Many prominent parallel veins. Glossy-green above, paler below; yellow in autumn. 6-8in (15-20cm).

Bark: smooth, dark brown, cracking into spirals in old trees.

Buds: pointed, red-brown, few scales. ¼ in (6mm).

Flowers: male catkins yellow, long, slender; female flowers round, green at base of male catkins which are often infertile.

Fruit: round, green, spiky fruits in bunches, containing 2 shiny, brown, edible nuts. 1½ in (3cm).

Shape: conical when young. Later, few large spreading branches form broad crown. Often coppiced.

A-Nut. B-Fruit. C-Flower spike.

It is not known when the sweet chestnut first came to Britain but it is thought to have been introduced by the Romans, like the walnut, for its edible fruits. The trees probably produced better crops than they do now as the warm conditions then prevailing enabled the nuts to ripen more often. Sweet chestnut grows in the southern part of the country and has naturalised itself on light soils there. Further north, although found in most areas, it has always been planted. As the tree is long-lived, old specimens can be seen in many parks and gardens. As sweet chestnut withstands shading, it was often grown under standards of other species, especially oak, as coppice in the south-east of England. Small areas are still managed in this way on a 12-year rotation for fencing stakes. The nuts provide food for many species of animals and birds, including squirrels, mice and pigeons.

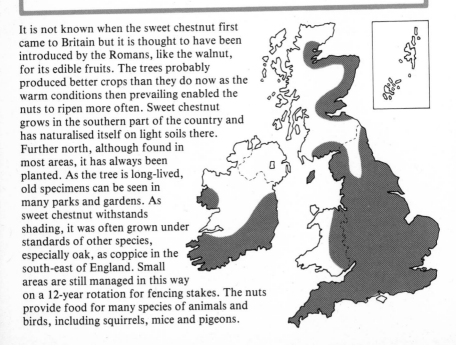

Wild Cherry

Prunus avium

Leaves: alternate; long, hang down. Sharp forward-pointing teeth. Thick, dull green above; paler, hairy below. Stalk has glands near base. Yellow-red in autumn. 2-6in (5-15cm).

Bark: shiny chestnut red, paler breathing pores in bands. Peels in horizontal strips.

Buds: ovoid, pointed, shiny brown, clustered. ¼in (6mm).

Flowers: males and females in same flower, clustered. Heart-shaped petals, open before leaves, May.

Fruit: round cherries, green, turn yellow, ripen red. Hanging on long stalks in pairs; bitter. ¾in (2cm).

Shape: young trees conical with even, rising branches. Older trees have broad, open crown.

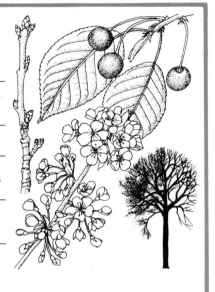

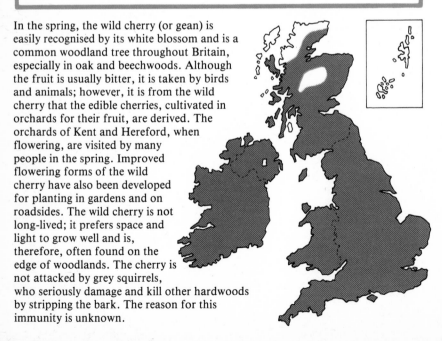

In the spring, the wild cherry (or gean) is easily recognised by its white blossom and is a common woodland tree throughout Britain, especially in oak and beechwoods. Although the fruit is usually bitter, it is taken by birds and animals; however, it is from the wild cherry that the edible cherries, cultivated in orchards for their fruit, are derived. The orchards of Kent and Hereford, when flowering, are visited by many people in the spring. Improved flowering forms of the wild cherry have also been developed for planting in gardens and on roadsides. The wild cherry is not long-lived; it prefers space and light to grow well and is, therefore, often found on the edge of woodlands. The cherry is not attacked by grey squirrels, who seriously damage and kill other hardwoods by stripping the bark. The reason for this immunity is unknown.

Bird Cherry

Prunus padus

Leaves: alternate; oval, thick, toothed. Bright green above, paler below; yellow-red in autumn. 2 glands on leaf stalk. 4 in (10 cm).

Bark: smooth, dark brown with orange breathing pores. Peels in strips; almond scented.

Buds: pointed, shiny, brown, like beech. ½ in (1 cm).

Flowers: males and females in same flower. Many white flowers in long, fragrant spikes after leaves emerge, May. Almond scented.

Fruit: small round cherry. Green, ripens red/black, August. ¼ in (6 mm).

Shape: small tree or shrub. Conical, slender rising branches when young; later branches spreading giving rounded crown. Suckers freely.

As a wild tree, the bird cherry is to be found only in the hilly woods of northern Britain where it grows high on the hillsides, up to 2000 ft (610 m). It is usually found growing with other trees which do not cast too dense a shade and it is often found in ashwoods together with wych elm on the limestone of northern England. Further north in Scotland, it occurs sporadically in birchwoods and also in the native Scots pine areas, especially by the sides of streams. The small cherries are bitter but are eaten by birds and the stones are dropped and spread by them. Bird cherry was among the earlier trees that re-colonised Britain after the ice ages. Garden forms of the tree have been developed which have larger and showier flowers and these have now been extensively planted in the south of England. Bird cherry can, therefore, be found throughout the country in gardens and on roadsides.

2000 BC

Walnut

Juglans regia

Leaves: alternate; 7 thick short stalked leaflets, terminal largest on longer stalk. Not toothed. Yellow-green above, paler below. Bronze in spring. 5 in (12 cm).

Bark: smooth, grey, becoming fissured into network of ridges.

Buds: ovoid, dull black, velvety. Vertically cut twig shows hollow pith with dividing layers. ¼ in (6 mm).

Flowers: male catkins yellow, tinged purple. Female catkins green, round, erect, at ends of shoots in groups.

Fruit: round, green with paler dots. Contains walnut, enclosed in wrinkled brown shell. 2 in (5 cm).

Shape: broad spreading open crown with twisting branches.

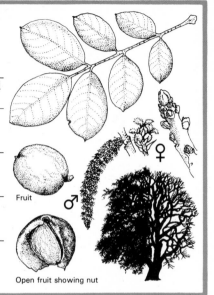

Fruit

Open fruit showing nut

The Romans are usually credited with the introduction of the walnut to Britain. The tree grows naturally in groves in southern Europe and had been in cultivation for its fruit for hundreds of years before the Romans invaded Britain. The climate of this country was warmer then than it is now, so walnut may have been more important as a source of edible nuts. Except in warm summers, the fruit only ripens regularly in the south and even then it is often taken by squirrels and birds before the nuts are ripe. The tree has naturalised itself in some areas in the southern part of the country and it can be found planted near houses, particularly farm houses, as far north as central Scotland. Although the tree has light foliage and an open crown, little grows beneath it. It requires plenty of space and a deep rich soil.

Holly

Ilex aquifolium

Leaves: alternate; oval, thick, sharp spiny teeth except high on tree. Dark glossy green above with pale margin, paler below. 1-4in (2.5-10cm).

Bark: smooth, grey-green when young; later silver-grey with fine cracks and warts.

Buds: small, ovoid, pointed, green. 2mm.

Flowers: males small, greenish white, 4 petals. Flowers in clusters. Females similar, with style, on separate trees in May.

Fruit: round berry, green, ripening red in dense bunches. Hollies with yellow berries also occur. ¼in (6mm).

Shape: small shrub or tree. Conical when young, spreading, rounded with age. Often sprouts at base of trunk.

Holly is the commonest evergreen tree to be found in Britain, occurring naturally in woodland but also planted extensively in gardens and hedgerows. In woodland it is often part of the understorey below the dominant vegetation of beech or oak, as it has the ability to thrive in the shade cast by these trees. This characteristic is often exploited when holly is planted as a hedge, as it can be used in shady situations where more exacting species would not survive. Its ability to withstand pollution makes it suitable for town planting, often in one of the decorative forms with variegated leaves that have been developed. It withstands cutting and can be clipped into ornamental shapes. The scarlet berries are eaten by birds but are often left until late in the winter when more palatable fruits have been taken.

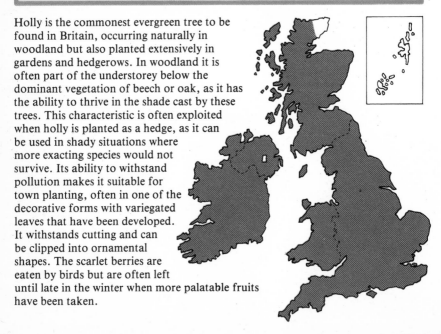

148

Hawthorn

Crataegus monogyna

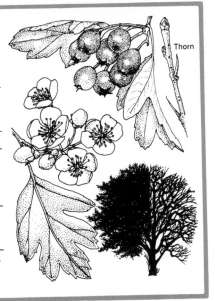

Thorn

Leaves: alternate; 3-7 rounded lobes, sometimes with double teeth, often without. Dark, shiny green above, paler below. Leaf-like stipules at base of leaf stalk. 3in (8cm).

Bark: orange-brown, cracks into squares. Bole fluted in old trees, often gnarled and furrowed.

Buds: small, brown, 2mm.

Flowers: males and females in same flower. 5 white petals with purple anthers. Many flowers in clusters. Open May, scented. Sometimes pink.

Fruit: round 'haw' with remains of calyx persisting. Green, ripens red. ½in (1cm).

Shape: small, much branched tree with rounded crown. When cut back, large leaves often produced. Thorny.

One of the most abundant small trees, hawthorn occurs nearly everywhere, even at high altitudes. It is a vigorous coloniser, soon invading any uncultivated or cleared area of land. The 'haws' are eaten by birds and the seeds spread in their dropping. The young seedling is protected by thorns preventing damage to it by browsing animals. If not cut back, hawthorn scrub soon covers the ground giving protection to other trees, such as oak, which grow up and eventually become the dominant vegetation. Because of its thorns and its ability to re-sprout and become very dense when cut and layered, hawthorn has long been used for hedges. Many miles were planted when land was enclosed, especially in the 18th century. Recently hedges have been removed to facilitate agricultural operations.

Woodlands of the Future

In Britain there is very little primary woodland left, that is, woodland growing on sites thought never to have been cleared by man. The largest such areas are the relics of the Caledonian pine forests in Scotland, remaining now in such places as Glen Affric in Highland and the Black Wood of Rannoch in Tayside. Some broadleafed primary woodland exists in southern England, such as the Wyre forest in Shropshire and the forest of Dean in Gloucestershire. All these relict areas, however, have been utilised for timber and forest products for many hundreds of years, and have been managed to some extent for this purpose. The area occupied by such woodland is small and totally inadequate to supply our timber needs, and so for generations we have imported very large and expensive quantities of timber and wood products every year. Britain no longer has an empire to provide these imports. The countries that used to supply them are developing themselves so that they need the timber at home, or to manufacture it into saleable articles for export, thus providing themselves with work and increased revenue. At the same time our other traditional suppliers, Canada, the United States and Scandinavia, are realising that their natural forests need conserving, while only the Soviet Union still has extensive untapped supplies.

Although there is no forest tradition in Britain, it has an excellent climate for growing trees, as they like the warm, wet conditions that occur here, particularly in western Britain. From Cornwall and Devon through Wales to western Scotland, there is land which is only marginally suitable for farming and it is only sensible to grow trees on it. As Britain's role in the European Economic Community develops, forestry will become more important. All European countries import timber but none as much as Britain, yet timber trees grow faster and better here than elsewhere in Europe and much faster than in Scandinavia.

There is room then for much more forestry in upland Britain and on a smaller scale in lowland areas, too, where woodlands can be integrated into farmland. It is more than fortunate that an expansion of forestry, so very desirable from an economic standpoint, can also provide both ecological and recreational benefits of immense value without detracting from the primary objective of wood production. There is no other industry, except perhaps the water supply industry (which can provide fishing, boating and birdwatching), that can enhance wildlife and recreation at the same time as providing a basic raw material, indeed one that is perpetually renewable, while at the same time improving the depth of soil.

Woodlands provide refuges for animals, birds and plants that cannot survive in towns, industrial areas and against modern farming practices. As a direct result of the increase of forestry plantations there are more deer in Britain now than ever before and a wider range of species. The fallow, sika and the little muntjac have all been added to Britain's wild fauna. The native red squirrel has retained its foothold in Britain in the pine plantations of East Anglia and a few other places. Pine martens, at one time almost extinct, polecats and wild cats are all increasing in coniferous plantations, adding exciting variety without any harmful effects.

Equally exciting is the successful re-introduction of the once-native capercaillie, the male bird of which is as large as a turkey, to our Scottish forests so that it has now become quite a common bird in Tayside. The crested tit, once a rarity, is increasing, too, in these same forests while the crossbill, previously confined to Scotland, is finding suitable habitats further south. The little firecrest from Europe is establishing a foothold as a breeding species in the new spruce forests in southern England and other species may well follow. It would be nice to see the Scandinavian pine grosbeak here and the jay-like nutcracker from Europe. Already the shy golden oriole has made attempts to breed in woodlands in southern England and the honey buzzard has a foothold, while the black woodpecker, common in deciduous and coniferous woodlands in western Europe, has only to cross the Channel.

Many species of animals and birds that are not woodland feeders still need woodlands as refuges to hide in and to breed, venturing forth when it is safe to feed in the surrounding areas. Woodlands, therefore, have a much wider ecological role than just for those species that are truly forest dwellers by habit. To some extent this is also true of plants. Although they cannot move out to the fields to feed, the last refuge of many plants are forest rides and woodland edges where they are not regularly disturbed by ploughing or heavily grazed by farm animals. Thus do red helleborine, twayblade, spotted-orchid, martagon lily and wild daffodils, to name just a few, survive in the woodlands. Many common species which are vulnerable to chemical sprays on roadside verges and in farmers' fields may only survive in woodlands in the future. Additionally there are many truly woodland flowers such as lady's tresses, spurge laurel and wintergreen as well as the more common bluebells, primroses and violets.

It is sometimes suggested that coniferous forests contain less wildlife than broadleafed woodlands, but there is very little evidence for this and the supposition is based more on a dislike of new and unfamiliar trees than upon fact. Animals and birds will make use of any suitable habitat and quickly adapt to any opportunities offered. While oakwoods are often quoted as containing a wide range of wildlife, it is forgotten that beechwoods, due to the lack of light filtering through the leaf canopy, are sparse in this respect. The British Trust for Ornithology, while looking at these two types of woodland and plantations of Norway spruce in the Chilterns, found more breeding birds in the latter than in beech but more again in oak.

The most important factors are age, not tree species and how long a tree has been growing here. Young oak and beechwoods do not provide good wildlife habitats any more than young conifer plantations. Indeed, as they grow more slowly, they remain in this uninteresting stage very much longer than rapidly growing conifers. Mature woods of both let in more light and have more dead material lying about, thus encouraging a variety of insects which in turn increases the bird population. In addition, the light encourages herbaceous vegetation which animals feed upon. Because we have not had conifer plantations in this country for long, few of them are mature, whereas many of our oak and beechwoods are old and decaying. It is easy to be misled by the disparity of age into a belief that conifers are poor wildlife habitats and broadleafed woods much better. To improve and pass on our natural heritage of wildlife as a whole, which includes flowers, we need more woodlands and as wide a diversity of them as possible. It is fortunate that there is an economic need for these woodlands for, without them, there would be scant resources to provide wildlife habitats.

As well as providing a wide range of habitats for wildlife, the forests of the future will increasingly provide a recreational resource of immense value. Our industrialised society has produced a population of which over 90 per cent lives in urban surroundings. There are material and social benefits derived from this which include increased opportunities for leisure activities. Urban living also generates a need to come in contact with natural surroundings. The 'wilderness' atmosphere of woodlands and forest provides for these needs in many ways. They can accommodate informal car, picnic and walking visits to the countryside much better than farmland where damage to crops and farm stock is always a danger. Woodlands and forests can absorb many more people than the open countryside and yet still provide solitude. Informal car parks can be provided in woodlands and walks arranged through them without significantly reducing the timber-producing capacity, and well-sited caravan sites need not be intrusive.

Forestry plantations can offer ideal facilities for orienteering, and motor rallies can be safer to the public and less intrusive if conducted on forest roads. Perhaps the greatest use of forests, after hikers, is made by horse riders but, while this is entirely compatible with growing timber, accommodation must be sought with walkers whose pleasure can be destroyed when paths are damaged by horses in wet weather. The quiet pursuits of birdwatching and observing animals are well provided for in forests of all types, particularly if there is diversity of ages and tree species.

While none of these recreational activities conflict with modern forestry practices, some understanding of the latter will enhance and add to visits to the countryside. What are they and how will they develop as our new plantations mature? The fundamental principle underlying forest management is 'sustained yield'. This means that the object is to go on producing a crop of trees and the timber they provide, permanently from a site. A simple example would be a 100-acre plantation on which the trees were allowed to live for 100 years and one acre was cut down and regenerated every year. So long as the site was uniform, a regular supply of timber would be provided indefinitely and there would always be one acre representing every age from 0 to 100 years. There are more sophisticated methods of forest management than this but the objectives are the same. For instance, in a woodland of mixed ages, the volume of timber that can be removed each year without reducing the overall yield, the 'allowable cut', can be calculated from growth records. Forest management thus involves continuous growth of the trees and regeneration of harvested areas. Regeneration can be by natural seedlings that have grown up under the mature trees before they were felled or which quickly fill the gaps left by felling. However natural regeneration, although aesthetically appealing, is difficult to ensure and often is very slow to form new woodland. It can be supplemented by planting additional trees; more often, no attempt is made to wait for natural regeneration and the whole area is replanted. Re-planting, or artificial regeneration, has many advantages. The first is that there is much more certainty of success and the second is that the whole area is utilised ensuring maximum use of the land. Additionally, there is an opportunity to plant young trees from genetically improved stock or even to change the species to include a more desirable one. Probably the greatest advantage is that much quicker early growth is achieved because the planted trees have been grown for two or three years in a nursery and are sturdy with well-developed roots. All these advantages of artificial regeneration add up to increase the yield from plantations over natural forests by about two-and-a-half times, and this will become more significant in the future as world timber supplies are expected to be outstripped by demand before the end of this century.

When the young forest has been established, after protection from browsing animals and weeding the young plants for a few years, it soon reaches the stage of 'closed canopy'. That is when the branches of the trees start to interlace as the trees grow outwards and upwards. From then on, the trees dominate the site and only very shade-tolerant plants will grow under them. At this time the amount of wildlife is at a minimum. Very soon the trees begin to compete with each other and, if they are to go on growing well, they need to be thinned out by cutting the poorer trees and allowing more light to the better ones. The trees cut out are usually large enough to be useful as stakes for fences and other small produce.

This process of thinning is carried out periodically for the rest of the life of the crop, always with the object of benefiting the best of the trees. The aim is to produce a final crop of excellent trees spaced evenly throughout the wood so that they all have an equal chance to grow. The selection of trees to be favoured at each stage is judged by eye but the amount to be removed is calculated from tables based upon the maximum yield of the site concerned. As soon as thinning starts and more light enters the forest again, wildlife is tempted to return and, in a mature forest with large, widely spaced trees and undergrowth, there is a variety of life exploiting the varied habitats provided.

Plantations are often of one species because they are easier to manage since two species do not often grow at the same rate. There is also usually a most profitable species for a site. This 'monoculture' can, however, have dangers as disease can spread more quickly. In the very long term the soil may be improved by a mixture of species or at least a change when the crop is harvested. When bare land is being planted for the first time, particularly if it is poor and exposed, which is the case on much of the new forest land in Britain, there are few choices as only hardy 'pioneer species' can be used successfully. These are light-demanders that are the first species to occur in a natural succession but they do not produce the high yield of timber that the more sensitive secondary species do. The latter are more tolerant of shade and can grow under other trees where there is protection from wind and the soil has been improved by the first crop. There will be an opportunity, therefore, to add to the diversity of our new forests in the second 'rotation' when the light-demanding pioneer species have ameliorated the soil with their leaf fall. It will always be wise not to clear large areas when the first rotation is harvested. This would be throwing away the valuable woodland conditions that have been created with regard to the soil, control of weeds and particularly shelter from wind, this last being the single most important limiting factor to tree growth in Britain.

Woodlands of the future will make use of the many successful introduced species, both hardwood and conifer, as well as native species and will be intensively managed to provide the timber and wood products that a highly industrialised society needs. At the same time they will be refuges for many forms of wildlife and provide a variety of relaxation and recreational opportunities. Familiarity with them, particularly with the trees they contain, will lead to their acceptance in the British countryside and perpetuate a varied tree heritage.

Glossary

Afforestation: the establishment of forest plantations on treeless land.

Amenity value: the aesthetic value of trees rather than their commercial value as a timber crop.

Anther: tip of stamen bearing the pollen.

Arboretum: a collection of specimen trees.

Arboriculture: the management of individual trees for their amenity value.

Arctic-alpine: plant occurring in the Arctic and on high mountains.

Aril: the fleshy cup that contains the seed of yew.

Axil: angle between leaf stalk and stem.

Bracts: modified leaves attached to flowers.

Burr: growth on base of tree.

Butt: the lower part of the stem of a large tree.

Cainozoic: period from the present day to 50 million years ago.

Calyx: the sepals surrounding and giving protection to the petals of a flower before it opens.

Canker: disease-damaged area of a tree, usually caused by fungus.

Canopy: the foliage of tall trees in a wood when this has interlaced to form continuous cover.

Carr: stage in succession from open fen to woodland.

Chlorophyll: chemicals in the green parts of plants required for the formation of food.

Climax vegetation: when stable vegetation cover is reached.

Conifer: a tree in which the seeds are borne in a cone

Continental climate: cold winters with hot dry summers.

Coppicing: cutting a tree back so that it sprouts from the stump.

Cultivar: cultivated form of a species.

Cuticle: thick covering of leaf which prevents drying out.

Deciduous tree: one that sheds leaves in winter.

Desiccation: excessive water loss, in trees usually as a result of drying winds.

Ecological succession: stages of vegetation cover, from bare land to climax conditions.

Ecosystem: all plant and animal life living in a particular habitat.

Evergreen tree: one that retains leaves in winter.

Exotic: any tree not considered a native.

Fastigiate: upward rising branches giving a compact tree crown.

Food chain: green plants eaten by animals, which in turn are eaten by other animals.

Grafting: propagation by uniting desired plant with a root-stock.

Habitat: conditions in which plant or animal lives.

Hardwood: a descriptive term used for the wood of broadleafed trees.

Heartwood: the inner wood in the stem and large branches of a maturing tree which is dead and provides rigidity but no longer conducts water and sap.

Hybrid: a cross, usually between species or varieties.

'Keys : a descriptive term used for the winged seeds of maple and ash.

Laterals: roots that run out from a tree horizontally a little below the soil surface.

Layering: propagation by rooting branches into the soil.

Leader: the terminal upward growing shoot of a tree.

Light-demander: a tree that requires plenty of light—a 'pioneer'.

Lignin: a chemical substance characteristic of the cell walls of wood.

Lopping: cutting branches off a tree.

Mesolithic: the age from 5000 to 9000 years ago.

Mesozoic: period 50 million years to 225 million years ago.

Monoculture: growing one species as a crop.

Naturalised: an introduced tree or plant that has escaped and now grows wild.

Neolithic: the age from 2000 to 5000 years ago.

Palaeolithic: over 9000 years ago.

Palmate: leaves that have lobes shaped like the fingers of a hand.

Pedunculate: fruits which are borne on a stalk (a peduncle).

Pioneer: the first plants to colonise bare land.

Policies: woodland round mansions in Scotland.

Pollarding: cutting trees so that they sprout at head height.

Pollination: carrying the pollen from the male parts of a flower, or from male flowers, to the female parts or to female flowers.

Propagation: regeneration of new plants by means other than seed, e.g. rooting cuttings.

Regeneration: the production of new individuals. In forestry 'natural regeneration' is the establishment of seedlings under older trees by natural seeding.

Ring bark: cutting round the bark and destroying the cells carrying the tree's food.

Root-stock: roots on which desirable grafts are grown.

Rotation: the period between planting and harvesting.

Sapwood: living wood in stems and branches through which water and sap flows.

Seed orchard: orchard where trees are grown for seed production.

Senile: elderly and beginning to decay.

Sessile: fruits which are not borne on a stalk.

Shade-bearer: a tree that will grow in the shade of others.

Species: a group of plants or animals that inter-breed.

Springwood: thin-walled cells laid down in stems and branches in the early part of the growing season.

Stamen: the male part of a flower which produces the pollen.

Standard: large tree left to grow for timber in coppiced woodland.

Stipule: leafy structure at base of leaf stalk.

Style: tip of ovary that receives pollen.

Succession: stages through which vegetation passes as conditions change.

Sucker: sprout sent up from roots of the tree.

Summerwood: thick-walled cells laid down in the middle of the growing season in stems and branches.

Variegated: foliage which has colours, usually yellow or white, in addition to green.

Variety: form arising in the wild, differing from the true species.

Index